Human Resource Management
in the
Leisure Industry

by
Peter Critten

LONGMAN

HUMAN RESOURCE MANAGEMENT IN THE LEISURE INDUSTRY

Longman Group UK Limited,
Westgate House, The High, Harlow, Essex CM20 1YR
Telephone: (0279) 442601
Fax: (0279) 444501

First published 1994

A catalogue record for this book is available from the British Library.

ISBN 0-582-233089

Printed by Page Bros Ltd., Norwich

To my wife Pino

in part compensation for months of leisure lost

Contents

Acknowledgements

This book would not have been possible were it not for the generous support received from the seven companies who were selected to illustrate aspects of good practice of HRM in the leisure industry. I am particularly indebted to the following people for their time (and that of their staff) and for the material they made so freely available to us:

Laurence Murrell, Managing Director of **Torquay Leisure Hotel Group**.

Tony Corfield, Director and General Manager of **Pleasureland** and Jill Corfield his wife and Personal Assistant.

Peter Keech, Personnel and Training Executive of **Butlins Southcoast World**.

Rob Whitehouse, Head of Recreation, and Lyn Brettle, Recreation Services Personnel Officer, **Borough of Thamesdown** and Jane Lewis, Centre Manager of **Oasis Leisure Centre, Swindon**.

Ken Heathcoate, Managing Director, and Karen Thorpe, General Manager, **Bolton Health Studio**.

Jan Hoy, Personnel Manager of **Beaulieu**.

Mo Heard, Manager of the Actors Company of the **Museum of the Moving Image (MOMI)**.

I am also grateful to Dave Lewis, Reader In Employment Law at Middlesex University, for comments on Chapter 2.

Introduction

In 1990 the Sports Council produced a summary report, 'Recreation Management Training Needs':[1]

> *A major theme was the need to change organisational cultures. There was a perceived danger in addressing education and training needs in an ad hoc and unstructured way without consideration of the values, aims and systems of the employing organisation.*
>
> *It was suggested that because of CCT, local government leisure services were shifting from a vague philosophy of public service to a more precise statement of aims, objectives and values. The bureaucratic and fragmented approach of local government needed to be replaced by a more coherent, integrative, organisational culture — one based on approaches and values described variously as 'consumer orientation', 'entrepreneurism', 'enterprise' or 'communal attitudes'.*

It concluded, 'Although often using some method of annual or bi-annual staff appraisal, many authorities lack a systematic staff development programme linked to the strategic needs of the organisation'. Human resource management puts the responsibility for selecting and developing staff to meet the strategic needs of the organisation into the hands of the line manager.

This guide aims to encourage managers in the leisure industry, in whatever sector, to take individual responsibility for ensuring that staff in their charge are provided with every opportunity to contribute both to the organisation's goals and to their own growth and development.

To facilitate this approach we have drawn on the experiences of seven organisations in different sectors of the industry which in their own way have taken steps to take a strategic approach to the development of their staff.

Three of the organisations, **Butlins Southcoast World**, **Torquay Leisure Hotel Group** and **Pleasureland**, have received the Government Investor in People award (*see* Chapter 10) which is recognition of the way they have linked individual development with business objectives.

Two of the organisations have received a National Training Award for the innovative way they have developed training methods to meet the needs of their particular industry — **Bolton Health Studio** and the **Museum of the Moving Image**.

Beaulieu and Bucklers Hard has been chosen to reflect how a single personnel policy embraces and integrates a very diverse range of visitor attractions (National Motor Museum, Abbey, Palace House, Maritime Museum and Bucklers Hard Village).

The seventh organisation, the **Oasis Leisure Centre** at Swindon (administered by **Thamesdown Recreation Services**), was the first leisure centre in Europe to be awarded BS5750 certification for quality assurance by the BSI. It is now in the process of reviewing its approach to staff development in preparation for an application for Investor in People (to be co-ordinated by Wiltshire Council). For a brief description of each organisation see the next section, Background on the case studies.

While we appreciate that many readers will be managers in the private sector and managers of facilities other than those found in a leisure centre (e.g. arts centre, leisure park), we hope that all readers will look upon the examples highlighted as *illustrative* of the kind of policies and initiatives *any* manager in the leisure industry can put into practice. We also appreciate there will be many organisations in the industry which will be disappointed that their own initiatives and policies have not been reflected in this guide. Clearly it cannot be representative of *all* the initiatives that have been taken in the industry. The seven organisations featured have been chosen for the above reasons to illustrate some general principles in human resource management. But it should also be noted that the examples of good practice attributed to each case study organisation are specific to them and would not necessarily be adopted by the other organisations represented.

HRM and leisure management

In the process of carrying out research for this book I had occasion to scan back numbers of *Personnel Management* and *Personnel Management Plus* (the journals of the Institute of Personnel Management) and the independent journal *Personnel Today* over the last three years and was surprised to find very few references to initiatives taken by the leisure industry.

References to personnel policy in the service industries tend to have been dominated by the NHS and banks and building societies, while the major oil companies and organisations like Rank Xerox and IBM tended to dominate in the private sector.

This is not to say, of course, as this guide hopes to demonstrate, that the leisure industry has not taken initiatives in the HRM field. But it may reflect how seriously the industry is taken as a national profession by other professions.

Leisure management is defined by Ralph Hebden in the Introduction to ILAM's *Guide to Good Practice in Leisure Management*[2] as being 'about managing the resources which people use to enjoy their free time'. One of those resources — some would say the most valuable resource — is the people who serve the people whose time is free. By definition, while serving the public this group of people is *not* free. While in the eyes of the public working in the leisure industry must be a 'fun' thing to do, two recent features in *Leisure Management* have focused on a rather different view of the industry from the inside.

In a salutary article entitled 'Working in leisure: delight or drudgery?',[3] Dr Bill Bacon identifies four factors in talks with leisure managers and supervisors which reflect the reality of current working practice:

- continuous shiftwork (which interferes with employees' own leisure time)
- long hours of work (average 55–60 hour week)
- jobs becoming more insecure (influence of CCT, cut back in local authority resources)
- stress.

This leads Dr Bacon to pose five questions for ILAM to address — questions to which we hope this guide will also respond:

1. Do entrants have unreal expectations of what leisure work is like?

2. How relevant are courses/education? Do they teach people how to cope with stress, boredom, difficult or abusive customers, poor managers, harassment, discrimination?

3. Is work in leisure, particularly the public sector, suffering a process of ongoing degradation in which the quality of the working experience is reduced, and if so, what are the consequences for the leisure and well-being of the people concerned?

4. Is leisure going to provide the growth in attractive job applicants which the huge expansion of college courses in the field obviously predicts?

5. Will the industry start to experience the problems of labour turnover (of the kind experienced by the hotel and catering industry)?

A more recent survey of ILAM members[4] reinforced the findings about levels of stress among leisure managers and concluded as follows: 'Most members realise that what they may in retrospect refer to as the "golden age" of the 1980s is gradually being replaced by a new, more frugal age. Most members are now working in an increasingly volatile and competitive environment.'

Of course, readers from other public services (notably the NHS) would conceivably recognise the above symptoms as being by no means unique to leisure services! But the fact that the issues have been articulated in the way they have gives the leisure industry an opportunity to respond.

It is interesting that one of the case studies at the centre of this guide, **Thamesdown Recreation Services**, was approached by a consultancy in stress management and persuaded to allow it to carry out a survey. A consequence of this survey was that Thamesdown recognised the value of giving staff the freedom to open up about personal issues, and now the Senior Personnel Managers make themselves available at an annual 'Staff Care Meeting' when staff can raise any issue of concern.

The principles and practice of human resource management, in our view, take a realistic view of the value of individual members of staff to an organisation while at the same time enabling those staff to develop competences that will make them equally valuable in the external labour market. We believe this approach is more appropriate to the 'increasingly volatile and competitive environment' in which the industry faces itself than the more traditional 'personnel management' approach which perhaps was suited to a more stable world where employees were expected to stay with a company for life and in return for loyalty could expect security of tenure.

While appreciating that managers are not personnel specialists, we believe it is important that you understand the shift that the HRM approach implies which is central to the issues raised in this guide. We also hope that this guide will be read by managers who are also students of HRM. There are innumerable references to articles in personnel management journals which can be followed up by those managers interested in pursuing these issues further. We hope that in this way more managers may recognise the relevance of HRM issues for them and equally how initiatives taken in this industry have much to contribute to HRM itself.

HRM and personnel management

The difference between HRM and personnel management is well described in this extract from a standard text for Personnel Managers:[5]

> *Personnel Management is* work-force centred, *directed mainly at the organisation's employees; finding and training them, arranging for them to be*

paid, explaining management's expectations, justifying management's actions, satisfying employees' work-related needs, dealing with their problems and seeking to modify management action that could produce unwelcome employee response...Underpinning personnel management are the twin ideas that people have a right to proper treatment as dignified human beings while at work, that they are only effective as employees when their job-related personal needs are met and that this will not happen without personnel management intervention in the everyday manager/subordinate relationships.

Human resources management is resource-centred, directed mainly at management needs for human resources (not necessarily employees) to be provided and deployed. Demand rather than supply is emphasised. There is greater emphasis on planning, monitoring and control rather than mediation. Problem-solving is with other members of management on human resource issues rather than directly with employees or their representatives. It is totally identified with management interests being a management activity, and is relatively distant from the workforce as a whole, as employee interests can only be enhanced through effective overall management....Underpinning human resources management is the idea that management of human resources is much the same as any other aspect of management and an integral part of it and cannot be separated out for specialists to handle.

Do you recognise these distinctions? Do you have a Personnel Management Department or a Human Resource Management Department? Does the difference matter?

There is still an ongoing debate about the difference among personnel specialists themselves. For some Personnel Managers it represents a threat to their very position taking away responsibilities for staff they thought should be theirs. For others it represents a welcome change for managers to take on responsibilities for staff development that are more business related and that enable them to change their role from trainers to facilitators.

The leisure industry, as our case studies reflect, is more characterised by personnel management than the HRM approach. Indeed, the Personnel Manager of one of the case studies, Jan Hoy of Beaulieu is herself the subject of a career book on what it is like to be a Personnel Manager.[6] She is introduced in the way many people see the Personnel Manager, as 'everyone's auntie'.

Our position is in no way to disparage the traditional 'mediation' role of the Personnel Manager between management and employee but to suggest that if Leisure Managers take an HRM approach (as this guide advocates) the role of the Personnel Manager is itself given greater value because:

Human resource management is essentially a business-oriented philosophy concerning the management of people in order to obtain added value from them and thus achieve competitive advantage'.[7]

But in answer to the critics of this approach, who see it as dehumanising people,[8] we would also have to say that the *only* way to get added value *from* people is to give value *to* them.

What the above definition omits to say is that HRM is also about releasing value *and power from* people which they might choose to use in ways other than for the organisation. The trick, of course, is to ensure that the needs and aspirations of the individual and the organisation are one and the same. This is achieved by commitment rather than compliance, which the old division between 'management' and 'staff' encouraged.

4

This division is very clear in the distinction made between personnel management and HRM by Torrington and Hall above.[5] Implicit in the power of the Personnel Manager of old is that there is little trust between staff and management. It is also rooted in a hierarchical structure of differentiated accountabilities. As we shall see, the shape of organisations are changing, as are working practices. In order to cope with the 'volatile environment' described above organisations must be more open to change from within in order to cope with changes outside. This in turn means less well-defined 'manager' and 'staff' roles. It is in the context of these changing values that this guide is written.

Structure of the guide

The sequence of ten chapters follows a step-by-step strategic approach which enables you to develop your own HRM policy. Fundamental to any HRM approach is having a clear picture of the purpose of your organisation which should be reflected in the values and culture your employees share; this should also determine the structure that best suits working practice. This is the subject of Chapter 1. Employment of anyone involves a legal contract; before we look in detail at specific HRM methods you are provided with a framework in Chapter 2 for reviewing the legal rights of each employee and your responsibilities within the law. Before employing anyone, whether on a full-time, part-time or seasonal basis you should read this chapter first.

Chapter 3 then helps you take a new look at the way jobs are defined in your organisation and how they can be redefined in competence terms and value added to them through National Vocational Qualifications. In Chapter 4 we look at how you can use a targeted approach to recruit and attract staff who will meet not just present needs but those of the future. Chapter 5 examines how the way you go about selecting staff is a basis for their future development, and says a lot about you as an organisation.

Chapter 6 is the most extensive in the book. Its theme is training and development, and continuous learning. It encourages you to look at your organisation as a place for continuous learning and improvement and lays the foundation for your assessment of your organisation against the 'Investor in People' criteria detailed in Chapter 10.

Chapter 7 helps you set clear performance standards for each job (building on Chapter 3) and establish a system for appraisal and evaluation covering all levels which can have an impact on the organisation as a whole. Chapter 8 then explores reward management, including the provision of a rationale for fair wage allocation and control and using a range of non-financial incentives to show you care.

Chapter 9 is another key chapter which is central to successful HRM — the need for a company-wide approach to communication which equally ensures all staff have the widest opportunity for involvement and participation.

The final chapter puts the previous nine chapters in the context of the Government's Investor in People award the criteria for which are included — and you are invited to measure yourself against each one aided by cross-reference back to source material in previous chapters.

In the Conclusion section at the end of the book we summarise the implications for a sound HRM policy for the future of the leisure industry and what the organisation of the future will look like.

A theme that runs through the guide is that to get value from people they must be encouraged to *act*, to carry out activities, and to achieve goals that are capable of being measured. You will also notice above that when we talk about 'staff' **you are included**. Therefore, as a result of completing this guide, we would expect you to add value to yourself which can be independently assessed and valued. At the end of the guide is 'an individual Action Plan' in which you will be encouraged to write up your own reactions, thoughts, plans and achievements as you work through each chapter.

Each chapter has been written in a standardised format of seven sections:

Section 1   introduces an idea/*principle* that sets the scene for the whole chapter.

Section 2   outlines the benefits of *what's in it for me?*

Section 3   outlines the background to the idea and *what's involved?* in applying it in practice.

Section 4   provides *examples of good practice* from the seven case studies to illustrate application of the ideas in practice.

Section 5   summarises *lessons to be learned* from the experience of the case studies.

Section 6   provides an *action plan* for putting the ideas into practice — a checklist of action points to be written up in your *action plan* at the end of the guide.

Section 7   provides a list of *references* to the ideas for those who wish to follow them up.

If you address the issues that are raised in each section of the guide and make plans in your individual Action Plan as to how to tackle them in your own organisation, you will have the basis for an HRM policy which could contribute to an application for the Investor in People award.

On a personal basis, evidence in your Action Plan (and further evidence it generates) could be used to get accreditation against NVQ Level 5 standards in Management (*see* Chapter 3) which relate to the recruitment and development of individuals and teams of people. Alternatively you can use relevant sections of the guide to help with particular problems/ issues you are faced with as a Leisure Manager — *see* the Index.

However you choose to use the guide, we hope it will help you to see your staff (yourself included!) in a new light, and will lead you to take and evaluate initiatives that will have a measurable impact on your enterprise as a whole. If they do we hope you will also write them up and share them with others and thus add to what we hope will be an increasing body of knowledge on HRM in the leisure industry.

References

1. Coalter, F. and Potter, J. (1990) *Recreation Management Training Needs — Summary Report* Centre for Leisure and Tourism Studies, Sports Council.

2. Hebden, R. (1992) Introduction *ILAM Guide to Good Practice in Leisure Management* Longman.

3. Bacon, B. (1991) Working in leisure: delight or drudgery? *Leisure Management* May 1991.

4. ILAM Survey (1992) How stressed are Leisure Managers? *Leisure Management* Oct 1992.

5. Torrington, D. and Hall, L. (1991) *Personnel Management* Prentice Hall.

6. Powling, C. (1990) *What it's like to be Jan Hoy — A Personnel Manager* Ginn and Company Ltd.

7. Armstrong, M. (1992) *Human Resource Management — Strategy and Action* Kogan Page.

8. Mant, A. (1992) Putting humanity back into human resources *Personnel Management* Jan 1992.

Background on the case studies

Beaulieu and **Bucklers Hard** are part of Lord Montagu's estate on the banks of the river Beaulieu in Hampshire. In 1952 Lord Montagu was one of the first owners of historic houses (Palace House) to open up his home to the public to help pay the maintenance costs. Following on from his father he continued to build up a collection of veteran cars which became the basis for the first National Motor Museum. Over the years a number of features have been added — a monorail and range of special features on the theme of transport. In addition visitors can visit Palace House and the ruins of the old abbey. Over 500,000 people visit Beaulieu each year.

Bucklers Hard, on the banks of the river, is a preserved ship-building village of the eighteenth century to which Lord Montagu added a Maritime Museum in 1962. It attracts 200,000 visitors a year.

Butlins Southcoast World at Bognor Regis, Sussex, was opened in 1960 and is one of five Holiday centres and six Hotels that form Butlins Ltd. Butlins became part of the Rank Organisation in 1972. It offers catering and self-catering holidays aimed at the family market with a range of leisure facilities including — aquasplash, fun-fairs, feature films, live cabaret, discos, bars, shops and a range of catering facilities. It can accommodate up to 6,500 visitors and 3,000 day visitors and in the peak season employs 1,300 people. It is the only holiday centre to be open all year.

Pleasureland is an amusement park at Southport on the North West coast. The park began operating just after the turn of the century. The local authority ran the park and granted leases to people to operate on the site. This went on until the 1980s when the authority decided to pass the task of rebuilding **Pleasureland** into a modern attraction onto the private sector. **Blackpool Pleasure Beach** was asked to take the lead lease on the site. At that time it operated around 25 per cent of the site, the other 75 per cent being independent tenants. Since then it has taken over control of many of the independents and now owns and operates on 75 per cent of the site. Rebuilding has not been limited to plant, equipment and infrastructure but encompasses the people side as well. The company currently employ 75 full-time staff with 270 seasonal staff employed from March to November.

Bolton Health Studios was established over 25 years ago and offers a range of facilities to members including two fully equipped gymnasiums, cardiovascular equipment, aerobics, sauna, whirlpool, skin-deep beauty salon, two squash courts and nut tree restaurant. It employs 26 full- and part-time staff.

The **Oasis Leisure Centre** operated by the **Borough of Thamesdown Recreation Services** was opened in 1976 and is noted for its three 'domebuster' water slides and fun lagoon pool with realistic waves and Caribbean water cascade. In addition it offers a range of other facilities (gym, sauna, squash, tennis, etc.) and conference venue. It employs 202 full- and part-time and casual staff.

The **Museum of the Moving Image (MOMI)**, part of the British Film Institute, was opened in 1988 to awaken popular interest in the moving image and its part in contemporary culture. Situated on London's Southbank adjacent to the National Film Theatre, the museum offers a live glimpse into six eras of the moving image with a company of 18 actors playing a part in time ranging from a Victorian Lanternist to an Odeon Commissionaire of the 1940s.

Torquay Leisure Hotel Group is a family-owned business which started in 1948 with just one hotel. Since then it has acquired three more hotels all adjacent to each other on a six-acre site in Torquay. The four hotels between them offer 400 bedrooms and apartments. Though a resort hotel, the aim of the MD is for an all year round business. It has therefore built up a range of leisure facilities including indoor and outdoor swimming pool, games room, indoor bowling rink, sauna and solarium, tennis courts, four ballrooms and extensive conference facilities. It employs 250 full-time staff.

1. What business are we in — mission, strategy, culture and structure

1.1 The principles

Human resource management is essentially a business-oriented philosophy concerning the management of people in order to obtain added value from them and thus achieve competitive advantage.[1]

There is no easy way to formulate personnel strategies which are business driven and which also recognise that ultimately it is people who implement the business plan…The important thing is to give an overall sense of purpose to HR activities which can provide the people the organisation needs and help them to understand where they are going, how they are going to get there, why certain things are happening and, most importantly, the contribution they are expected to make towards achieving the company's projected future growth and prosperity.[2]

By definition, if the organisation does not have a business strategy which is clearly articulated and communicated to all it cannot practise HRM. So, the starting point must be for you first to ask the question, 'What business are we in?' and then to go on to ask, 'How does this affect and how is this influenced by the way we select and develop our people?'

This chapter will seek to help you answer the first question. The rest of the book helps you answer the second.

1.2 What's in it for me?

1. 'If you don't know where you're going you won't know when you've arrived.' How can you assess and improve the contribution of your staff if there are no criteria against which to measure their achievement?

2. Your success as a manager is increasingly likely to be judged against your ability to demonstrate how you have enabled your staff to contribute to *organisational* and not just department goals. The purpose of management has been defined by the industry lead body for management standards (the Management Charter Initiative — see Chapter 3) as 'To achieve the organisation's objectives and continuously improve its performance'[3]. Recently the lead body setting standards for *Personnel* Managers declared that the purpose of Personnel is to enable 'management to enhance the individual and collective contribution of people to the short- and long-term success of the enterprise'.[4] So, however you define your management role, in some way it must add value to the organisation as a whole.

3. If your company intends to be considered for the Government award 'Investor in People' (see Chapter 10), the first criterion you must meet is 'to make a public commitment from the top to develop all employees to achieve its business objectives'[5]. This commitment is measured in two ways:

> *Every employer should have a written but flexible plan which sets out business goals and targets, considers how employees will contribute to achieving the plan and specifies how development needs in particular will be assessed and met.*

> *Management should develop and communicate to all employees a vision of where the organisation is going and the contribution employees will make to its success, involving employee representatives as appropriate.*

1.3 What's involved?

Let us start by being clear about what we mean by 'mission', 'strategy', 'values', 'vision', etc., which often tend to be used as if they were synonymous:

- mission is about **purpose** — or what business we are in
- objectives are about **strategy** — or how we will get there
- vision is about **values** — or what really matters.[6]

There's one more term to add — **'culture'**. This has been popularly described as the 'way we do things around here'.

> *Culture is the commonly held and relatively stable beliefs, attitudes and values that exist within the organisation.*[7]

We can now bring all these terms together if we take an example of an organisation that has had a powerful influence on the way the leisure industry is perceived and on how it has organised itself, for example Disney. Walt Disney had a *vision* of an enterprise as a world of fantasy where the dreams, images of the young (and not so young!) could be realised. This became the guiding *mission* of Disneyworld the business of which was to create and make this dream world real. Its *strategy* for doing so was to see its staff not as employees but as 'actors', 'creators' and to train them rigorously to perform a role. Once at work they were cast on a stage. Anyone joining Disney couldn't help but be caught up in the *culture* which was the embodiment of these values. They do have rigorous training but it is the culture, reinforced by every contact and working relationship, that ensures Disney remains consistent to its values and mission statement.

You can no doubt think of household names in this country that have a very definite image in the public's mind, not only because of the business they are in but *how* they go about that business: Marks & Spencer (commitment to quality/customer service), The Body Shop (commitment to animal-free products, concern for the environment). This vision is reflected in the company culture.

A useful typology for identifying different types of culture was developed by Charles Handy (with Roger Harrison) and is described in his book *Understanding Organisations*[8] which also includes a useful questionnaire you can use in your own organisation to find out which of the following culture types your organisation falls into:

1. Power culture — very much the one-man (or woman!) rule-and-divide culture where one person is at the centre of the organisation (rather like a spider at the centre of a web). All decisions have to be referred to this one person. This type often originates from a family-run business.

2. Role culture — essentially the bureaucratic model as reflected in a typical organisation chart. Clear distinctions of ranks; everyone knows their job and sticks to it but can be promoted from one level to higher one. This type typically reflects public service (Army, police, NHS).

3. Task culture — here a task or project is the central focus rather than an individual role or rank of authority. Good examples can be seen in Chapter 9, e.g. teams specifically formed to solve particular problems (i.e. quality). We shall see that many organisations are currently in a transition between a role and a task culture.

4. People culture — an unusual and potentially 'anarchic' organisation where each person is treated equally and valued for their expertise. By definition no one can have coercive power over another. The kibbutz or small professional group or 'cluster' are examples.

The very different cultures have distinct *structures*, whereby their values are communicated and reinforced. These range from the spider in its web, via the typical hierarchy to what is known as a 'matrix' organisation where staff from different departments and different ranks can come together to solve joint problems. Finally, the 'person' culture can become operational in the form of a 'loosely coupled organic network' in which groups of people can be contracted by a central core group to achieve a particular task. Three of these models are illustrated in Figure 1.1.

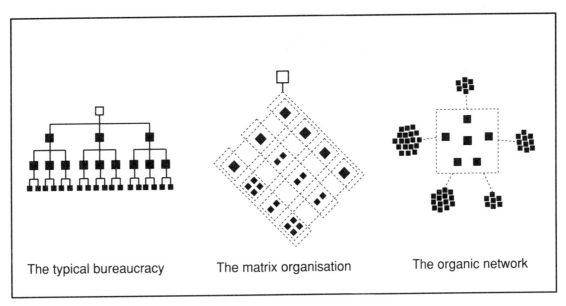

The typical bureaucracy   The matrix organisation   The organic network

Figure 1.1 Types of organisational structure

The structure of staff accountability in most of the case studies falls into the hierarchical role model. But there are times when interdepartmental groups come together to achieve specific tasks (e.g. related to health and safety, and quality — see Chapter 9). A question to consider is, to what extent could model three become the norm in the future? At the moment much of the industry takes on regular seasonal staff (see Chapter 4). Consider the viability of contracting regular trained groups to operate almost as autonomous sub-groups (e.g. with responsibility for particular rides and facilities).

The concept of the 'flexible firm' has been around for some time[9] and the need for 'flexibility' to cope with an ever changing market place is a key theme of the book. The flexible firm is one where there is a stable number of people at the *core* with varying numbers at the *periphery* who are employed for varying lengths of time depending on changing needs. The leisure industry seems to fit in very well with this model.

Finally, have a look at Figure 1.2, which is a mission statement for the organisation of the future which embodies many of the values we will be exploring in this book.

Our company faces competitive world markets and rapidly changing technology. We need the flexibility to add or delete products, open or close facilities, and redeploy the workforce. Although we cannot guarantee tenure in any particular job or even future employment we will work to ensure that all our people are fully employable — sought out for new jobs here and elsewhere. We promise to:

- *Recruit for the potential to increase in competence not simply for narrow skills to fill today's slots.*
- *Offer ample learning opportunities, from formal training to lunchtime seminars — the equivalent of a month a year.*
- *Provide challenging jobs and rotating assignments that allow growth in skills even without promotion to 'higher' jobs.*
- *Measure performance beyond accounting numbers and share the data to allow learning by doing and continuous improvement.*
- *Retrain employees as soon as jobs become obsolete.*
- *Recognise individual and team achievements, thereby building external reputations and offering tangible indicators of value.*
- *Provide three-monthly sabbaticals or external internships every five years.*
- *Find job opportunities in our network of suppliers, customers and venture partners.*
- *Tap our people's ideas to develop innovation that lower costs, serve customers and create markets — the best foundations for business growth and continuing employment.*

Source: 'Creating a habitat for the migrant manager' Keynote address by Ros Moss Kanter at 1992 IPM National Conference from 'Personnel Management', October 1992.

Figure 1.2 Mission statement for the organisation of the future

1.4 Examples of good practice

Not all of our case-studies have a mission statement and strategy linked to specific action plans. Some, like **Butlins' Southcoast World**, for example, put the emphasis on 'guiding principles'. While others, notably **Thamesdown Council**, have a clear mission statement and strategy for each of their leisure centres.

The Oasis

Thamesdown Borough Council has defined a mission statement for leisure in the community:

To promote and achieve an improved quality of life for all residents, irrespective of their ability and circumstances, through the provision of an extensive range of facilities: recreational, and artistic activities; and aesthetically pleasing environment, together with professional expertise and support.

This then breaks down into strategic aims, each of which is broken down into specific policies, for example:

Strategic aim	Policies
LE4. To provide a support infrastructure to ensure quality is provided in an efficient and effective manner and which reflects good value for money to the local community.	A. To develop a uniform and consistent approach to support services, especially in the areas of finance, administration, information technology and purchasing, with specific emphasis on financial awareness and cost effectiveness. B. To identify staff needs to ensure staff are able to reach their maximum potential through training and an awareness of the corporate strategy.

Each leisure centre is then invited to agree targets for which it is responsible to meet specific policies, who is responsible for meeting them, and performance indicators. Figure 1.3 presents **Oasis**'s service plan to meet strategic policy LE4B.

Actions/targets/service standards	Responsibility Recreation site services	Performance indicators
To provide awareness of corporate strategy through involvement in staff training	Personnel and Training Training Officer	90% of staff trained
To implement the appraisal and staff development scheme to all staff by June 1993	Personnel and Training Assistant Head of Recreation	Scheme implemented
To review staff training needs on an annual basis in March each year	Personnel and Training Training Officer	Training needs established
To assist with the introduction of NVQs to recreation services	Personnel and Training Training Officer	Reports generated
To provide training programmes and facilities trainees placements	Personnel and Training Training Officer	Number reports facilitated

Figure 1.3 Extract from OASIS service plan

In this way individual accountability for corporate strategy can be established and appraised (see Chapter 8).

Torquay Hotel Group

Since taking over the management of the hotel business from his father in 1981, MD Laurence Murrell had a vision of developing a range of accommodation and leisure facilities to 'generate income and employment all year round, not just in the summer months'. His strategy for realising this mission was to purchase additional hotels adjacent to the first hotel, install a range of leisure facilities and to make these facilities available to all residents of the four hotels.

Facilities currently include:

- mediterrania indoor pool
- outdoor pool
- games rooms
- indoor bowling rink
- sauna and solarium
- spa pool and coffee shop
- two tennis courts
- croquet lawn
- children's adventure playground
- extensive conference facilities
- five ballrooms (dancing holidays is a key feature).

The four hotels between them offer 400 bedrooms, in addition to which there are 36 self-catering apartments. The MD is under no illusion that to meet his objective of 'a full house 365 days of the year', *all* staff have to be clear about the business strategy and their responsibilities for achieving it. Furthermore, the communication of the plan to all staff was a key factor in the company acquiring Investor in People status.

A full account of this process is described elsewhere.[10] Figure 1.4 contains an extract of how the MD ensured his vision was communicated down to all staff.

Figure 1.4 How Torquay Leisure Hotel Group communicates their mission and strategy to all staff

1. The Business Plan was 'cascaded' down from MD to the General Managers who each produced a 'Hotel Operational Plan' which in turn went to Departmental Heads who produced their own departmental plans which in turn were communicated to all departmental staff. The final stage was for an individual development plan to be drawn up for each member of staff when they were appraised. In this way there was tangible evidence that the development of each employee was linked to the overall business plan.

2. Individual hotel General Managers were made responsible for particular targets (sales etc.). Specific action plans were drawn up for achievement of these targets and publicly displayed to staff in all the hotels. Below is an extract from the company action plan on sales:

Sales

Co-ordinating responsibility: L Murrell

To maximise company sales by developing an awareness of and responsibility for sales with all employees so that sales are established as one of the main company priorities.

Particular emphasis and development to be given to the roles of reception, management and other front of house staff in sales and the need for a team approach to sales.

Contd.

Figure 1.4 contd.

		Who	When	Progress
1.	Introduce regular company sales meetings of key personnel responsible for sales from each hotel to develop and co-ordinate hotel sales activities (two to three monthly).	I Murrell V Hinchcliffe	June	Ongoing
2.	Ensure sales results (level of bookings etc.) are promptly fed back to managers and receptionists.	V Hinchcliffe	July	Ongoing
3.	Ensure sales information is included in all departmental and management meetings.	Hotel management teams	Ongoing	Ongoing

3. Monthly newsletter (features guests and staff).

4. Annual presentation by MD to which *all* staff are invited. On the last occasion the MD gave presentation on two separate dates to allow staff on duty to attend on alternative dates. This gives MD an opportunity to review the past year and present the agenda for the coming year. It also gives staff an opportunity to comment.

Butlins Southcoast World

The 'happy campers' image of the post-war Butlins has long since changed since the merger with Rank (in 1972) and the complete redevelopment and transformation of five existing 'camps' into five Holiday Worlds. The objective is to provide on one site and for an inclusive price accommodation, hospitality, entertainment and leisure facilities for all members of the family. As the brochure says 'It's your chance to swim together, play together, eat together and laugh together'. But at the same time specialised facilities are available for toddlers, youngsters, teenagers, and adults of all ages.

There is no mission statement as such. Instead each employee at induction gets a copy of 'Guiding Principles' which are 'a statement of best practice for managers and staff alike, plus a reminder that this is a dynamic business with commercial goals'. The principles emerged from the 1990 Management Conference where Butlins' MD laid down these guiding principles to 'motivate the management team into new achievements and a new people-centred (customers and employees) management style.

It is an interesting set of values which on the one hand still embraces a very clear line of accountability while on the other looks for a 'creative, lateral thinking workforce' who are encouraged to 'seek new opportunities and to review existing practice'. The inevitable release of energy often conflicts with existing policy which needs to be openly confronted and acknowledged rather than controlled (*see* Chapter 9).

Beaulieu

The tourism and leisure business at **Beaulieu** *has been the 'engine' powering the costly conservation of its historic buildings and countryside for 40 years. Few* *properties have been so successful in harnessing and guiding this demand so as to enhance the enjoyment of visitors and benefit the community, the environment and the precious places that the visitors seek.*

The **Beaulieu** Estate (encompassing **Bucklers Hard**) is unique among our case studies. Though it has received a number of awards for the development of staff, unlike other examples it is not seeking an Investors in People award or National Training award. It doesn't have the same kind of 'mission' or core values we have so far examined for three other companies in our case studies. The key to its success and, as we shall see, what characterises the way its staff are developed is that it has always set the standard based on a set of unique assets rather than by responding to changing demands of the public.

When the present Lord Montagu inherited the **Beaulieu** Estate in 1952 and made the historic decision to open up his family home and estate to the public it was done for one reason — to ensure the estate and all its historic sites were preserved. This central aim is made very clear to new staff in the Induction Handbook:

> *Activities at Beaulieu and Bucklers Hard today are many and varied but it must be remembered that all individual activities serve one over-riding aim, namely: To ensure the continued existence and continual enhancement of the Beaulieu Estate as an entity in family ownership, an area of outstanding beauty and an integral part of the New Forest and to make appropriate areas of the estate accessible to public enjoyment.*

The key to success of this venture is also made very clear — visitors are our business.

Being inducted into the '**Beaulieu**' experience is a cross between being received into a family and serving an old-style apprenticeship. The notion of 'targets' cascading down the organisation would not fit the **Beaulieu** way of doing things. Much more in tune with its 'values' are the Thursday lunch of bread, cheese and wine to which all department heads are invited from *all* enterprises that make up the estate to informally 'chat' and share experiences.

But nevertheless there is a very tangible culture which all share which begins at Induction (*see* Chapter 4). The culture is such that, in the words of the Personnel Manager, 'people come and go very quickly or they stay forever'.

Museum of the Moving Image (MOMI)

MOMI is part of the British Film Institute and was formed in 1988 to directly attract a wide popular audience to appreciate the power of the 'moving image' and its impact on contemporary culture. In its first year it won the British Tourist Association's award for Best New Tourist Attraction.

What is unique about its employees is that they are all actors. This was **MOMI**'s way of providing security guards who would at the same time 'enliven specific areas in which visitors find themselves and to inform and entertain'. Rather like Disney every employee has a particular role (such as Hollywood journalist in the 1930s or Victorian lanternist). Each role (*see* Chapter 6) requires an employee to absorb as much as they can about the history and culture of the times in which their role is set so that they can literally bring it alive to every visitor.

This 'mission' and culture require a very particular kind of actor who is committed to the concept while being able to interpret their role in a very individual way.

1.5 Lessons to be learned

1. Each organisation defines its business and communicates its purpose and values to its employees in very different ways. At the one extreme is the **Oasis Leisure Centre** whose strategy is determined by the local authority and is divided up according to individual accountabilities; at the other end of the spectrum is **MOMI** and the **Beaulieu** Estate which regards its employees as part of an extended family and expects them to behave as such. But, however different the mission, strategy and values, a new employee would have a clear picture of what the organisation stands for and how they are expected to contribute to its aim.

2. This picture is conveyed to *every* member of staff. Again the methods will vary (*see* Chapter 9), but every member of staff is updated on company objectives and their role in achieving them.

3. Opportunity for staff to feedback — at least two of our case studies have realised the importance of enabling staff to feedback their comments on plans/strategies coming top-down. Every year Laurence Murrell, MD of **Torquay Leisure Hotels**, takes the opportunity to address employees of all four hotels about company's plans and to take on board their comments. At the **Oasis**, Senior Personnel staff sit down once a year and informally chat with staff about the plans for the centre and invite their comments. These are fed back to the manager of the centre who has to respond with an action plan, to be included in the following year's Service Plan.

We look at the power of two-way communication in Chapter 9.

1.6 Action plan

Turn now to the Individual Action Plan at the back of the guide and under headings in Chapter 1 write down your response to the following action points:

1. Write down in one sentence the purpose of your organisation: 'The purpose of my organisation is to...' Try and be as specific as you can, e.g. 'The purpose of my organisation is to provide the facilities of a leisure pool to the local community with the particular aim of encouraging disabled people to use our facilities.'

2. Ask each member of your staff to do the same. This is best done in small groups of six to eight. If possible you should introduce the exercise but you might choose to do it via your departmental heads who in turn pose the same question to their staff. The object is to get each group to arrive at a common statement. The separate statements are then combined.

3. Ask each member of staff in appropriate groups to think about what kind of organisation they are. What makes it special to work here? How would they hope a new member of staff would describe working here after one week?

4. After an initial warm-up discussion ask each member of staff to write down individually on cards provided five values. Collect the cards and try to arrive at a common list of five core values that summarise responses, e.g.:
    — 'We're very friendly.'
    — 'We take care of our customers.'
    — 'We go out of our way to help, particularly the disabled.'
    — 'We enjoy and take delight in the facilities ourselves as much as do the visitors.'
    — 'We all share a concern for the community and for encouraging more locals to use our facilities.'

5. Put together all five values in a single statement which is a vision of what it is like to work for the company:

    All our staff have a dual commitment to the community, especially the disabled, and to helping as many people from the community experience and enjoy our facilities to the full.

    You now have a purpose (mission statement) and a description of what your staff value most about working for you. You may well be surprised by the response, you may well not share their picture of your organisation. But without this information you won't be in a position to change their views (if that is necessary), nor be able to recruit and develop staff to create the organisation you wish to become.

6. Now consider which of the four culture types or combination of types best characterises the way your staff work together.

7. Finally, which of the model structures in Figure 1.1 best enables your staff to work together to achieve this mission.

1.7 References

1.   Armstrong, M. (1992) *Human Resource Management — Strategy and Action* Kogan Page.

2.   Cooke, R. and Armstrong, M. (1990) The search for strategic HRM *Personnel Management* December 1990, pp.30-33.

3.   *National Vocational Qualification at level 5 in Management* (1992) BTEC.

4.   Sieff, D. (1993) Defining the purpose of personnel *Personnel Management Plus* Vol. 4, No. 9, September 93, p.11.

5.   Employment Department (1991) *Investors in people — the Route* Employment Department, Moorfoot.

6.   Leigh, A. (1988) *Effective Change — Twenty Ways to make it Happen* IPM.

7.   Williams, A., Dobson, P. and Walters, M. (1989) *Changing Culture — New Organizational Approaches* IPM.

8.   Handy, C. (1985) *Understanding Organisations* Penguin.

9.   Critten, P. (1993) Investing in people to becoming a learning organisation *ILAM Guide to Good Practice in Leisure Management* Chapter 3.3, Longman.

10. Atkinson, J. (1984) Manpower strategies for flexible organisations *Personnel Management* August 84.

2. Rights, responsibilities and procedures

2.1 The principles

So far we have been able to discuss HRM from a purely strategic point of view with regard only to its impact on the organisation — which is its prime focus. But as soon as an organisation *employs* someone, i.e. enters into a contract with them to remunerate them in exchange for use of their skill and experience, there are *legal* implications.

There are some 30 Acts of Parliament that regulate staff relations and employment — 50 per cent have been passed in the last two decades. A list of the key Acts is given in Figure 2.1.

---

1. Sex Discrimination Act (1975).

2. Race Relations Act (1976).

3. Health and Safety at Work Act (1974) and Control of Substances Hazardous to Health COSHH (1988), and Management of Health and Safety at Work Regulations (1992).

4. Equal Pay Act (1970).

5. Employment Protection Consolidation Act (EP(C)A) (1978).

6. Wages Act (1986).

7. Trade Unions — key acts:
   — Trade Union Reform and Employment Rights Act (1993)
   — Trade Union and Labour Relation (Consolidation) Act (TULRCA) 1992.

Figure 2.1 Significant legislation affecting employment

At the time of publication the most current is The Trade Union Reform and Employment Rights Act which came into force in August 1993. The Act amends previous legislation regarding *when* employees should receive written particulars of their job. Any employee required to work for more than eight hours a week will be entitled to a statement within *two months* of starting work (previously it was thirteen works).

The number of hours worked each week is what determines an individual's rights under the law:

1. People who work fewer than eight hours a week have few rights.

2. People who work for at least eight hours but less than 16 hours a week get benefit of all statutory rights when they have been in employment for five years.*

---

* At the time of going to publication a ruling by the House of Lords on a case brought by the Equal Opportunities Commission gives part time workers unfairly sacked or made redundant the same rights as full timers to compensation or redundancy if they have worked for the same employer for *2 years*.

3.   People who work at least 16 hours a week are treated alike in the eyes of the law whether they work 16 or 40 hours a week.

Translating this into more recognisable working practice: a full-time member of staff would work every day the 'normal' hours stipulated by employer (e.g. 9am–5pm) all week, all year round (with holidays as agreed in contract of employment — *see* below).

Part-time is an arrangement less than above, i.e. less than normal hours but if an employee works 16 hours a week they are entitled to full rights (NB Britain has more part-time workers than any other EC country (6 million).

Casual/temporary — less than a month, less than eight hours a week

Though it *has* been the practice to classify staff in this way this may not be the case in the future. We have already identified the changing structures of organisations which are having to adapt to change outside and, as we shall see throughout this book, from inside. Flexibility is the key word. This means full-time work is unlikely to be the norm. Indeed less than 50 per cent of employees have traditional 9am–5pm jobs. Many want to work part-time to suit domestic arrangements (women with young children for example). In 1991 part-time workers made up 22 per cent of total employees. By the year 2000 that figure is expected to rise to 25 per cent.

We have already introduced the concept of the flexible firm, with a small core of full-time employees and two other groups, one part-time the other contracted for their skills when they are needed. In this respect the contracting of seasonal staff by much of the leisure industry reflects the kind of working arrangements which will be more common in the future. But what is important is that the industry *recognises* the value of these staff and affords them the *same* legal rights as its full-time employees.

Indeed, those of our case studies that use seasonal staff, **Beaulieu**, **Butlins Southcoast World** and **Pleasureland**, encourage them to return each season — which enables them to capitalise on the initial training provided. Indeed, in the case of **Butlins Southcoast World**, which is open all the year, there is a trend to offer a career progression route.

This chapter is not intended to make you an expert on employment law but to outline what individual employee rights are now and to discuss trends for the future (now that we are all part of a European Common Market). What is crucial is that you understand the ethos within which these laws have emerged — because it must have an impact on the way your employees perceive their role at work. As a result I hope you can use this information to shape your employment policy for the future.

The aim is to help you take an essentially *strategic* view of employment in so far as legislation is concerned; not to regard it as a constraint on your business but as a factor you can use positively in defining an HRM strategy for your company. In fact after reading this chapter you may want to add dimensions to your mission and vision in so far as how your company seeks to protect and enhance employee rights. It should also influence the way you recruit and contract staff to cover the competences you will identify in Chapter 3.

2.2 What's in it for me?

1.   You have legal obligations as an employer.

2.   You can turn what might seem legal 'constraints' on your freedom as an employer into ways of enhancing the value of your organisation.

3. You have an opportunity of anticipating the future, going beyond the requirements of the present.

4. Laws have implications for the social context within which people work and addresses many of the issues we shall raise in Chapters 8 and 9.

5. The basis on which you can write your staff handbook.

2.3 What's involved?

In this chapter we look at legal implications under seven key headings, each of which should be the basis for *strategic* decisions. At the same time we look at the procedures a company should establish which are open to both employer and employee to use to ensure that a standard of employee relations is maintained. The seven headings are:

1. Contract of employment.

2. Equal opportunities and discrimination.

3. Special provision for maternity rights.

4. Health and safety.

5. Unfair dismissal and redundancy.

6. Trade unions — recognition and rights.

7. The EC Social Charter and implications for the future.

There is also, I hope, a rationale in their order. The starting point is a contract of employment. From then on a key right underpinning much of legislation is the right not to be discriminated against. Items 3 and 4, above, relate to special provisions to be made for a safe and healthy working environment with particular reference to women's rights. Item 5 is another fundamental right, not to be unfairly dismissed and the rights of employees if they have to leave employment through being made redundant. Item 6 is another basic right, for every employee to be a member of a trade union. Finally, we look at some of the implications for the future as laid out in the EC Social Charter.

Under each heading we summarise key issues and refer to appropriate legislation. You are also advised to follow up issues raised through general references.[1,2] Finally, as you work through each section you may want to make notes in your Action Plan which reproduces each of the following headings as a check list for action.

1. Contract of employment

According to the Employment Protection (Consolidation) Act (EP(C)A) (1978) an employee is defined as 'an individual who has entered into or works under...a contract of employment'. A contract, by definition, has to include an offer and acceptance of employment and can be verbal. But the Trade Union Reform and Employment Rights Act of 1993 stipulates that all employees working eight hours or more must be given written particulars about their job within two months of starting. Furthermore it stipulates that the following information *must* be included in one document:[3]

- Name of employer and employee.
- Date when employment began.
- Date when continuous employment begins.
- Scale of rate of remuneration or method of calculation.
- Intervals at which remuneration is paid.
- Terms and conditions relating to hours of work (including normal working hours).
- Holiday entitlement including any entitlement to accrued holiday pay.
- Job title or brief job description.
- Place of work.

This is the basis for the legal contract and could well be included in the offer letter. In addition the remainder of the information may be provided in instalments, so long as this is done by the end of the second month:

- Terms relating to sickness, injury and sick pay.
- Pensions and pension schemes.
- Period of notice each party must give to terminate the contract.
- Where the employment is temporary, how long it is likely to last or the termination date of a fixed-term contract.
- Collective agreements which directly affect terms and conditions.
- Where employees are sent to work outside of the UK for more than one month, details of period outside the UK, the currency in which they will be paid, special benefits when working abroad and terms relating to their return — all must be given before they leave.
- Disciplinary and grievance procedures (unless there are fewer than 20 employees).

Many of the details of this supplementary information could well be part of a company handbook— *see* below and case study examples.

2. Equal opportunities and discrimination

Every employee has the following legal rights to safeguard their being discriminated against. Discrimination can take two forms:

- Direct — where one person is treated less favourably than another on one of prohibited grounds (e.g. sex, race). Thus sexual harassment would come under this category.
- Indirect — where a minority group is penalised by implication (e.g. change in conditions in time-keeping which might affect minority group or domestic arrangements).

Grounds for discrimination covered by law are as follows:

1. On grounds of being or not being a member of a trade union — (Employment Act 1990).

2. On grounds of sex, pregnancy or maternity — (Sex Discrimination Act 1975 and Equal Pay Act 1970).

3. On grounds of race — (Race Relations Act 1976).

4.   On grounds of 'spent' criminal record — (Rehabilitation of Offenders Act 1974).

5.   On grounds of being disabled — (Disabled Person Acts 1944 and 1958) Under these Acts organisations with more than 20 employees must ensure that at least 3 per cent of their workforce comprise registered disabled people. Furthermore Company Regulations of 1980 require companies of more than 250 people to make a statement as to a company's policy towards the disabled during last financial year in terms of training, career development and promotion.

6.   Assertion of a statutory right (EP(C)A 1978).

Not covered by law but increasingly an area of concern and one on which you should have a policy is discrimination on the grounds of age and sexuality. AIDS is another instance where there is no legislation but on which you should have a policy (there is a DE guide available).

You should ensure that your employees are clear about your policy on equal opportunity and discrimination and the procedure they should take if they feel they are being discriminated against. An extract from **Pleasureland's** employee handbook is shown in Figure 2.2.

Company policy on discrimination

It is the company's policy not to victimise or discriminate, either directly or indirectly against anyone seeking employment or in its employ, on the grounds of colour, race, ethnic or national origins or on the grounds of sex or marital status.

You are reminded that it is a breach of the Race Relations Act or Sex Discrimination Act to discriminate against another person on the grounds mentioned above. This principle will apply in respect of all conditions of work including pay, hours of work, holiday entitlement, overtime and shiftwork, sick pay, recruitment, training, promotion and redundancy.

Any form of such unlawful discrimination in recruitment of employees, or in the course of an employee's employment with the company, will not be tolerated and will result in normal disciplinary procedures (listed in section 10). If you consider that you are suffering from such victimisation or discrimination you should make a complaint under the grievance procedures (listed in section 11).

Figure 2.2 An extract from Pleasureland's employee handbook

3. Special provision for maternity rights

From October 1994 women employees will have the right of 14 weeks maternity leave, regardless of hours worked, or length of service under provisions made in the Trade Union Reform and Employment Rights Act (1993). In effect this takes on board the EC Maternity Directive passed in October 1992. A woman can decide when the 14 weeks should begin as from the 11th week before the expected week of childbirth. During this time her contractual conditions remain unaltered and she will receive special maternity payment the details of which still have to be agreed at the time of publication.

Under EP(C)A (1978) a woman has the right of return to work up to 29 weeks after the week in which the baby was born.

With the change in law on maternity rights being extended (to any form of working) the Equal Opportunities Commission anticipates an increase in claims under the Sex Discrimination Act.

4. Health and safety at work

The Health and Safety at Work Act (HASAWA) of 1974 is important because it places the onus for health and safety at work on the employer 'to ensure, so far as is reasonably practicable, the health, safety and welfare at work' of all of their employees. This includes health and safety in relation to:

- provision and maintenance of plant and systems of work
- arrangements for use, storage and transport of articles and substances
- maintenance of place of work and access to and exit
- working environment.

In particular you have a responsibility to:

- provide adequate welfare facilities
- provide necessary information, instruction, training and supervision
- consult with union safety representatives (if there are any)
- display a notice giving the main provisions of the Act.

Clearly in the context of the leisure industry with its range of attractions and facilities the issue of safety is critical. Inspectors empowered to enforce the Act operate on behalf of the Health and Safety Executive and have far-reaching powers. If an accident occurred on your premises one of the first things such an inspector would check is that any operator involved had received appropriate safety training in the operation of whatever facility was involved. All of our case studies, for example, provide regular training sessions and updating of employees in all aspects of safety.

It is also important to impress on every employee *their* responsibility for safety and for ensuring all accidents are reported systematically in an Accident Book (major accidents leading to death and minor accidents leading to incapacity for more than three days need to be reported on a standard form) One way of ensuring the health and safety message gets to everyone is through the company handbook. In Figure 2.3 is the extract on safety contained in **Beaulieu's** staff handbook.

The handbook is also a convenient way of getting across to all employees their responsibilities under two other legal requirements:

Any establishment in which more than 20 people are employed requires a fire certificate under The Fire Precautions Act of 1971. A requirement of getting a certificate is that all employees have been instructed in use of fire extinguishers and fire drill (including arrangements for evacuation).

Hazardous substances were the subject of the Control of Substances Hazardous to Health (COSHH) Regulations of 1988. This is important for another reason. Unlike HASAWA which requires employers to take 'reasonably practicable' steps to ensure safety of their premises, COSHH starts by requiring employers to carry out a 'risk assessment' of tasks where employees could be exposed to hazardous substances. As a result they then have to outline a plan as to how risks can be controlled and minimised. This has particular relevance to swimming pools, for example, where a range of chemicals are used.

The carrying out of 'risk assessment' is likely to be a requirement for all aspects of health and safety in the future as a result of an EC 'Framework Directive' which has no less than nine Directives in force before the end of 1993 (seven of them by January 1993).[1,4] They cover assessment of risk in following areas: asbestos, biological agents, workplace (in general), use

---

Health and safety at work

You share with your colleagues a responsibility for the safety of yourself and others. The exercise of common sense will ensure that you do not allow your place of work to become dangerous to yourself, other staff or visitors.

Employees will:

1. Acknowledge that it is a condition of their employment that they must comply with all general safety provisions and specific safety practices concerning their job at all times and that failure to do so will make them liable to disciplinary action.

2. Take care for the health and safety of themselves and of persons who may be affected by their acts or omissions at work.

3. Co-operate as is necessary to ensure that any statutory duty or requirement or company procedure is complied with.

4. Wear any personal protection provided as a result of specific regulations or company requirements and use appropriate safety devices at all times.

5. Report accidents, near miss occurrences, damages, defects or potential hazards to their immediate Supervisor, Safety Representative, Head of Department or Safety Officer.

6. Adhere to all instructions given by the Safety Officer and others with responsibility for health and safety.

Figure 2.3 Example of health and safety policy from staff handbook provided by Beaulieu

of work equipment, issue of personal protective equipment, manual handling of loads, display screen equipment, carcinogens, temporary workers.

If you have clear policies under HASAWA most of these areas should be covered (except you will be required to formally produce a written risk assessment in all of these areas). A particular area of concern within the leisure industry might be the Directive relating to manual handling of loads. This entails an employer identifying tasks of manual handling where there is a risk of injury. If possible other forms of automated handling would be introduced; but where manual handling is unavoidable an assessment should be made of size of load, working environment (space, lighting) and individual capability and appropriate information and, where necessary, training provided.

At the moment these Directives have not been included in health and safety legislation. It is perhaps not surprising, therefore, that a survey carried out three months after eight of the Directives should have come into force found 54 per cent of companies failed to meet requirements.[6] However, that is no reason why you should not take account of them in your overall HRM strategy.[4]

5. Unfair dismissal and redundancy

Every employee has the right not be unfairly dismissed under EP(C)A (1978). However, over the last 14 years there has been a gradual raising of the qualification period for claim of unfair dismissal from six months (to which labour Government had reduced it in 1979) to two years (as it now is) on grounds that it takes that length of time to assess acceptability. An employee who has two years of continuous employment can take their case to an Industrial Tribunal which will determine whether the employer had established a *fair* reason for dismissal and whether the employer acted *reasonably*.

Fair reasons include the following:

1. The capability of the employee: the use of clear standards of competence — see Chapter 3 — will help define levels of competence/incompetence.

2. The conduct of the employee: there are certain offences which automatically count as 'gross misconduct' and fair grounds for instant dismissal. These include:
   — theft, fraud or deliberate falsification of records
   — fighting or assault on another person
   — deliberate damage to company property
   — incapability through alcohol or illegal drugs
   — serious negligence which causes unacceptable loss, damage or injury
   — serious acts of insubordination
   — working for a competitor or damaging company's commercial interests.

3. Redundancy (dealt with separately below).

4. Contravention of statutory duty or legal restriction preventing employee from doing job: for example, loss of driving licence where employee needs to drive as part of job.

5. Some other substantial reason (SOSR): usually in connection with unilateral changes, reorganisations of the business (though a Tribunal would want to see evidence of prior information and consultation)

The key to whether dismissal of an employee is fair or unfair lies in the interpretation of *what is reasonable*. One of the best guidelines in this matter is the Code on Disciplinary Practice and Procedures in Employment published by ACAS, the Advisory, Conciliation and Arbitration Service.[6] ACAS was established as a statutory body under the Employment Protection Act of 1975. Its role was revised under the Trade Union and Labour Relations (Consolidation) Act of 1992 (TULRCA). Its general duty is 'to promote the improvement of industrial relations' and to assist in resolution of trade disputes through conciliation and arbitration.

If you had dismissed one of your employees on what you believed were fair and reasonable grounds and the employee took you to an Industrial Tribunal, the court would take into account the following to determine whether your action was *reasonable*:

- following consultation and proper disciplinary procedure, including carrying out a reasonable investigation
- being consistent in the application of discipline
- that the disciplinary action was appropriate to the particular case
- taking into account any mitigating circumstances (e.g. long service, good record, provocation, domestic or personal problems).

To help employers develop a standardised and fair system within which they could make judgements about dismissal, the Code laid out a system of three stages to be followed after which dismissal would follow. This has been the basis on which companies now operate and is clearly indicated in the staff handbooks of our case studies. In Figure 2.4 is the Disciplinary procedure from **Pleasureland's** Staff handbook.

Normal disciplinary procedure

Before you are subject to any disciplinary action you will be invited to attend a hearing at which you will be told how your work or conduct falls short of the expected standard, what that standard is, how long you have to bring your work or conduct up to standard and what the consequences of failing to do so will be.

You will be given the opportunity to state your case, and if the hearing is held in connection with disciplinary procedures under the third or fourth stage (below) you will have the right to be accompanied by a fellow employee of your choice.

The stages of normal disciplinary procedure are:

The first stage — oral warning
  This stage will be applied in cases of unsatisfactory work or of a minor breach of conduct. A note outlining what took place at the hearing will be given to you as soon as possible after the hearing.

The second stage — written warning
  This stage will be applied in the case of a second instance of unsatisfactory work or minor breach of conduct, or in the first instance of misconduct which is of a serious nature but which falls short of gross misconduct as defined below. The written warning will be given to you as soon as possible after the hearing.

The third stage — final written warning
  This stage will be applied in the third instance of unsatisfactory work or minor breach of conduct, or in the second instance of misconduct which is of a serious nature but which falls short of gross misconduct. The final written warning will be given to you as soon as possible after the hearing.

The fourth stage — summary dismissal
  This stage will be applied in one of the following circumstances:-
  — the fourth instance of unsatisfactory work or minor breach of conduct
  — the third instance of misconduct of a serious nature
  — the first instance of gross misconduct.

Figure 2.4 Example of disciplinary procedure from staff handbook provided to permanent staff at Pleasureland

With such a clear statement of policy and procedure any manager at the company should be able to implement dismissal procedure, if required, in a fair and reasonable way.

There is one instance of 'fair' dismissal which we need to address separately, redundancy. Redundancy is defined by the EP(C)A (1978) as a dismissal which is 'attributable wholly or mainly to': an actual or intended cessation of business, or an actual or expected diminution in requirements of business either generally, or in the place in which the employee is employed. It is management's prerogative requiring only evidence of need for fewer employees. But if a company is unionised, employers would be expected to consult with unions about proposed redundancies *before* they are announced as to how dismissals could be avoided and their consequences mitigated.

Given the need for 'downsizing', most companies would seek to avoid compulsory redundancies by considering other ways of reducing staff. These are some examples:

- early retirement
- natural wastage and/or non-filling of vacancies

- reducing or eliminating overtime working
- reduction in basic weekly hours (through negotiation)
- redeployment or transfer of employees (with provision of necessary training)
- terminating employment of temporary employees
- reduction, elimination of subcontracted work
- voluntary redundancies.

In the event of need for compulsory redundancy it is good practice for the employer to state just what is their policy on selecting people for redundancy. One procedure is 'Last in First Out' (LIFO) which is often thought to be fair by unions and employers alike. On the other hand it does not always serve the best interests of the company. **Pleasureland's** policy on redundancy, extracted from the 'Permanent Employees' Handbook', is shown in Figure 2.5.

In the unfortunate event that it becomes necessary to institute a programme of redundancy the main criterion for selection of those chosen must be 'to serve the interests of the company'.

We have never operated a 'last in, first out' policy, and each department must retain those staff whose skills and productivity will enable us to function most effectively in the future.

Selection for redundancy will be based on an assessment by your Department Manager taking into account factors such as those listed below:
— productivity and efficiency of the job
— attendance record
— disciplinary record
— team commitment
— adaptability to changes in working practice.

2.5 An extract from Pleasureland's policy on redundancy

If made redundant an employee over 18 and under 65 (or normal retiring age) has the right to statutory redundancy payment provided they have been continuously employed by the employer for two years and more. Employees on a contract with less than 16 hours a week are excluded unless there have been five or more years of continuous employment at eight hours or more. Statutory redundancy payment is calculated by taking the number of years employment (in age ranges under 22, 22–40, 41 and over) and multiplying by the appropriate number of weeks pay (maximum level of weekly pay is counted). No employment beyond 20 years is paid so the maximum amount is 20 x 1.5 (rate for employees over 40). Since 1 April 1992 the maximum weekly amount has been £205.

Of course, as an employer, you can choose, as many employers do, to offer a more attractive redundancy scheme. This also signals to the workforce the value you place on them. What is more the kind of support service you offer employees facing redundancy will also reflect the culture of care you operate. Unfortunately during this last recession, redundancy has affected all levels of staff in all kinds of companies. During the last decade a new term has emerged 'outplacement'—the opposite of recruitment, helping employees facing redundancy to find a job in the external market. Many companies use established consultancies to offer such a service to employees. Some companies, like Marks and Spencer, have developed their own in-house service.[7]

The redundant employee has a statutory right to time off to search for another job but this should be the absolute minimum service offered. In addition you should offer a range of other services of which these are examples:

- individual counselling
- services of a professional outreachment agency
- funding of specialised training.

Just as the way you recruit staff says a lot about your HRM policy so does the way you deal with employees who have to leave whether through their own fault or through no fault of their own (redundancy).

6. Trade Unions — recognition and rights

Under TULRCA (1992) every employee has the right to belong (or not belong) to any union of their choice irrespective of previous agreements (i.e. with particular unions). On the other hand the employer has the right to recognise (or not) an independent union when it seeks recognition rights to represent employees' interests.

We don't propose to elaborate further on the rights of unions because only you will know whether your establishment/company has an agreement with one or more independent union. From an HRM perspective, it must be accepted that unions have a part to play in representing the collective interests of employees but equally, as we continually emphasise, it is important that as a manager you have the right to communicate directly to individuals. However, you may decide that there are benefits in standardising procedures under some form of collective agreement to which there is usually strong commitment on the part of the workforce.

An interesting example of a company that has managed to combine recognition of a union (in this case a *single* union) with HRM practices like flexibility and direct communication is the Japanese company, Nissan.[8]

7. The EC Social Charter and implications for the future

The EC Social Charter was introduced to create a 'level playing field' between very diverse countries with very different employment policies; the fear was that those with lower employment standards would take advantage to expand industries at the expense of those with better employment standards. It was adopted at the Strasbourg Summit in 1989 (despite Mrs Thatcher's protests) and makes provision for a range of social and employment rights:

1. **Freedom of movement**: To enable people in the community to move freely within its borders to 'engage in any occupation or profession in the Community in accordance with the principles of equal treatment as regards access to employment, working conditions and social protection in the host country'. This has implications; for example, for recognition of qualifications from member states (e.g. NVQs — *see* Chapter 3 and the provision of the same conditions of employment to subcontracted workers from other member states as those for domestic workers. These issues are still under debate by the Council of Ministers.

2. **Employment and remuneration**: This seeks to ensure that all workers receive 'an equitable wage' *regardless* of whether they are part-time, temporary or full-time. Note that it *doesn't* propose a binding minimum wage, but merely commits members to a non-binding pledge to ensure that all workers have a 'decent standard of living'.

3. The Commission has produced draft-directives applying to 'atypical' workers (i.e. part-time or temporary) proposing that they get access to vocational training, that they get [pro-rata] rights on social security benefits, dismissal payments, holidays, pension schemes and equivalent access to health and safety as full-time workers. As you can imagine some of these are less likely to be opposed by the Government than others. But this should not stop you formulating your own policies for services you can provide.

4. **Information, consultation and participation for workers**: Legislation on employee participation is anathema to the current British Government and even in the EC has been fraught, but in 1990 the Commission produced a draft directive for the establishment of European Works Councils. These would be made up of members elected/appointed from the workforce for information and consultation on company policy (though applied to companies having at least 1,000 employees in the EC with at least two establishments in different member states). It is recommended representatives be informed of progress of business and its prospects, details of production and sales, employment situation and possible trends, and investment prospects. Also that representatives be consulted on any management proposal likely to have 'serious consequences' for employees' interests. There are also non-binding recommendations on profit-sharing and financial participation. We shall look at these issues in Chapters 8 and 9.

5. **Protection of children and adolescents**: The aim is to prohibit employment — other than light work — for those below school-leaving age (or in any case under 15). It also seeks to ensure that young people in work are protected in terms of pay, hours of work and access to training.

6. **Elderly persons**: The aim is that everyone retiring from work should have a decent standard of living. Since this is usually provided by pensions and social security systems under the control of separate member states, little action has been taken.

7. **Disabled persons**: This seeks to improve the integration of those with disabilities into work and society through training, ergonomics, better accessibility and mobility and changes in housing. A draft Directive on Mobility of Handicapped Workers was issued in February 1991.

8. **Health and safety at work**: More has been achieved in this area than any other because it is covered by the Single European Act. We have already looked at its provision under health and safety above.

Though Britain has opted out of the Social Charter it will still be subject to EC Directives from the Single European Act (to which Britain is signatory). Also, many British companies already operate throughout Europe. Will their employees in member states be excluded from provisions catered for in the Social Charter? Also, will their experience of employment policy in Europe have an influence on culture in the parent company in the UK much as Japanese employment practices have had an effect on changing management practices in this country? The issues of the Social Charter are likely to dominate the agenda for employment standards in the 1990s and within your overall HRM strategy you should make provision for accommodating them.

This concludes our survey of seven areas where you will be required to review and/or establish the direction your own company will be taking when we come to the Action Plan.

Where appropriate we have made reference to procedures that support particular legal requirements (e.g. four-stage disciplinary code).

But there is a common procedure that should be open to all employees to raise any *grievance* they have whether in relation to the seven statutory areas or any mother matter concerned with employment. Again, it is usual for grievance procedures to be detailed in the staff handbook.

The form a grievance procedure takes is usually to encourage the employee to resolve it with their supervisor in the first instance and thereafter with succeeding heads (depending on extent of the hierarchy). A caveat is usually added that the employee should expect a written response to their grievance within *seven days*. A paragraph that summarises the procedure in **Beaulieu's** staff handbook is shown in Figure 2.6.

Should you have any grievance relating to your employment, you should speak to your immediate superior and explain the situation to them. If you and your superior cannot reach a solution satisfactory to you both you may then take the matter to your superior's Head of Department. If the matter is not then resolved it may then be taken to the Managing Director whose decision is final (unless he decides to refer the matter to arbitration). At any level you may be represented by anyone of your choice whether or not an employee of the company, and the company also has the right to be represented by anyone of the company's choice.

2.6 Summary of Beaulieu's grievance procedure

Of course, though the MD might have the final say from the company's point of view the employee has the right to take the matter to an Industrial Tribunal if they still feel dissatisfied.In practice the very existence of such a procedure is usually sufficient for most disputes to be resolved in-house.

2.4 Examples of good practice

Throughout the last section we have referred to extracts from the staff handbooks of some of our case studies. The staff handbook is the means of conveying both statutory rights as well as in-house information. We don't propose to give further detailed extracts but to indicate the range of type of handbook that you might want to provide.

In general more information is given to permanent staff than is given to seasonal staff. The format is also rather different. Typical of the kind of brochure given to seasonal and all staff is the A5 glossy with graphics and cartoons from **Butlins Southcoast World**. This is its contents:

- welcome to Butlins
- the Butlins' Story
- the five Holiday Worlds [other similar establishments]
- stars [training system — see Chapter 6]
- careers in Butlins
- personal appearance
- your accommodation
- you and your wages [explanation of wage slip]
- leisure facilities [on site]
- the who's who of Southcoast World [followed by map of site]

- places to go off centre
- some important points [covers hours of work, absence, working extra hours, your mail, staff pass, telephones]
- when you leave
- solving problems [grievance procedures, discipline procedure, do's and don'ts]
- Food Hygiene Regulations 1970, how they affect you
- preventing fires
- what to do in the event of a fire
- use of fire extinguishers
- Health and Safety at Work Act [reference to examples of safety practice].

In all cases the information is appropriate to the target population — seasonal staff. It raises issues which are then elaborated upon in induction. This is in contrast to **Pleasureland's** handbook for full-time staff which is much more formal and detailed. Its contents are as follows:

- message from Managing Director
- Mission Statement and Training Development Policy
- the history and background of Blackpool Pleasure Beach
- the history and background of Pleasureland
- hours of work, lateness and absenteeism
- salaries
- holidays
- company pension and life assurance schemes
- absence from work including company sick pay and private health scheme
- maternity pay and maternity leave
- employment legislation — your rights under law and company policy
- personnel records and references
- disciplinary rules and procedures
- grievance procedures
- safeguarding company property and the right to search
- use of telephones
- health and safety
- accidents, safety and company policy on the use and abuse of alcohol, drugs, and other substances
- staff amenities
- leaving the company.

2.5 Lessons to be learned

1. The staff handbook can be used for a number of purposes:
   — to provide personal welcome/introduction to the company
   — to provide some basic information about company and its facilities
   — to focus on key issues to be picked up in training
   — to inform employee of statutory rights and procedures for safeguarding them.

   The question is whether it can do all of these things at the same time. You will have an opportunity to explore this for yourself in the Action Plan.

2. Some of our case studies did not have staff handbooks as such but nevertheless had specific procedures relating to most of the seven areas we've covered. The point at issue for the future, as Directives from Europe have an increasing impact, is how companies will *integrate* such a complexity of data in such a way that it can best be communicated to a variety of types of employee. (*See* Chapter 8.)

2.6 Action plan

In your Action Plan for Chapter 2 you are asked to carry out two audits following on from the themes introduced in this chapter.

1. Review the mix of staff currently working for you and existing contractual arrangements for employment under the headings given.

2. Against each of the legal headings we have examined indicate how well your present arrangements meet the legal criteria (as discussed in section 3) and note what changes need to be made and how best they can be communicated to staff.

2.7 References

1. Towers, B. (ed) (1992) *A Handbook of Industrial Relations Practice: Practice and the Law in the Employment Relationship* Kogan Page.

2. Lewis, D. (1994) *Essentials of Employment Law* IPM (4th edition).

3. Aikin, O. (1993) Particular requirements *Personnel Management* August 1993.

4. James, P. (1992) The health and safety agenda *Personnel Management* March 1992, p.23.

5. Lowe, K. (1993) Firms turn blind eye to health and safety *Personnel Today* 23 March, p. 1.

6. ACAS (1977) *Code on Disciplinary Practice and Procedures in Employment* HMSO. *See also* ACAS (1987) *Discipline at Work* ACAS.

7. Crofts, P. (1991) Helping people to face up to redundancy *Personnel Management* December 1991, pp. 24–27, 45.

8. Wickens, P. (1987) *The Road to Nissan* Macmillan.

3. Redefining jobs and competence at work

3.1 The principles

The 'job description' has traditionally defined the boundaries of an employee's role within an organisation structure and broadly the tasks they will be expected to perform. Traditionally written by the Personnel Department, reflecting the duties required by a particular department, it has been the basis on which most of the decisions about an employee have been based directly influencing:

- recruitment
- selection
- contract of employment
- training
- appraisal
- job evaluation (and subsequent level of remuneration)
- disciplinary procedures.

It also has a legal status in so far as, as we saw in Chapter 2, it is the right of an individual to have a written statement giving details about the job. The Trade Union Reform and Employment Rights Act, which came into effect in August 1993, amends previous legislation regarding *when* employees should receive written particulars of their job. Any employee required to work for more than eight hours a week will be entitled to a statement within *two months* of starting work (before it was thirteen weeks).

But there is nothing in law which stipulates the form the description should take. The right, a reasonable one, is that any employee has a *written* statement which defines the broad outlines of the job. It us up to the employer just *how* the employees' responsibilities are defined.

An example from one of the case studies is seen in Figure 3.1.

Job descriptions differ in the amount of detail they provide. In the main they indicate:

- the title
- accountability (to whom/for whom)
- a summary of the duties, tasks to be undertaken
- breakdown in detail of main responsibilities.

Some will also give details of the working conditions (workplace, facilities, salary, etc.) and standards against which the performance of the employee will be evaluated.

While it is acknowledged that the job description provides useful information about the current role in my view it is more suited to organisations from the past (bureaucratic in structure) operating in a stable climate where there are clearly defined roles which are unlikely to change. In Handy's classification of culture (*see* Chapter 1) it is more suited to power and role cultures. On the other hand, as we also saw from Chapter 1, the organisations of the future need to be flexible, and have the capability of adapting quickly to change outside. This means they need structures and systems on the inside that can change. Job descriptions by definition do not lend themselves easily to such change.

Designation	Activity Assistant
Group	Arts and Recreation
Division	Recreation
Section	Oasis
Grade	4* Permanent and qualified
	3* Probationary and/or unqualified
Responsible to	Activities Manager

Responsible for — With others, the provision of a safe and efficient, comfortable and enjoyable service to customers using the facilities of the centre.

— Keeping an up-to-date and appropriate first aid and pool life saving qualification approved by the council.

Main duties/responsibilities:

1. To be responsible for the safety and conduct of the public in the leisure pool including Domebusters while on duty in the pool and to maintain the rules set out by management regarding the behaviour of the public in the pool hall and the surrounding spectating areas.

2. To be responsible for and maintain the cleanliness of the pool hall, pool surrounds and the glass areas and pool furniture, the swimming changing areas, the showers and toilets, the dry changing rooms and all the sports facilities, and any other areas of the centre as required, using the appropriate chemicals and powered machinery provided.

3. Supervision of the public in the wet changing area, checking the public through the control point into the pool including token exchange for flume mats and general supervision and assistance to the participating public during activities including rollerskating and other parts of the centre including security of building and equipment.

4. To be responsible for maintaining, setting up and taking down all sports and major event equipment including outdoor facilities and other items of furniture when necessary. Check all equipment is in safe working order and report to the Duty Officer/Supervisor any which does not reach the required standard.

5. To provide the public with information about the centre as and when requested. This may include facilities and special programmes available and how they go about using the facilities and equipment available.

There are an additional 12 duties listed.

Figure 3.1 Typical job description (Oasis Leisure Centre)

But there has to be *some* statement of what an employee is required to do at any given time. There has to be a way of describing the range of skills you will need to realise the mission you have set yourself. But, in the same way as we have suggested an organisation's mission will need to change, together with associated values, so the way we describe people's *functions* has to be just as flexible.

In fact, by concentrating on *functions,* we shift the focus from tasks and procedures to the purpose and outcome of work activity. This is the basis of a revolution that is currently going on which will have wide-ranging implications for all aspects of HRM. It involves a nation-wide reassessment of the standards of all occupations in this country from the point of view of what people at work actually have to *achieve* to be *competent* at a particular job or occupation:

> *The concept of competence...is defined as the ability to perform the activities within an occupation or function to the standards expected in employment. Competence is a wide concept which embodies **the ability to transfer skills and knowledge to new situations within the occupational area. It encompasses organisation and planning of work, innovation and coping with non-routine activities. It includes the qualities of personal effectiveness that are required in the workplace to deal with co-workers, managers and customers.** [1]*

The aim is to establish a system of National Vocational Qualifications (NVQs) based on *competence*, i.e. how people actually perform in the workplace, and to give all employees the opportunity to demonstrate competence in their own workplace. By doing so they can not only demonstrate their ability to their employer but get accreditation which is recognised *nationally*. Furthermore each NVQ is assigned a *level* to reflect its complexity and the degree of initiative, responsibility involved. This ranges from 1 for routine work (operator level) to level 5 which involves application of complex techniques across a wide and often unpredictable range of contexts (management).

The main change is the move from describing jobs in *input* terms (i.e. tasks, procedures to be carried out) to what has to be achieved in *output* terms.

If you have ever used an existing job description for the purposes of selection, or for designing a training programme you will recognise the inefficiency of job descriptions to give you a specific picture of what an employee has to achieve. Translating job descriptions into profiles of competences on the other hand gives you a direct link between individual contribution and the organisation's *purpose*. As we shall see later, the way you go about describing contribution in terms of competences is first to ask the fundamental question: What is the *purpose* of this job, occupation, profession?

You will have an opportunity to ask this question of a range of occupations in your organisation and work through the procedure called 'functional analysis' to break down a job into its key competences each of which can be directly linked to your organisation's mission. As your mission changes so will the competences you need.

The way you describe a particular occupation can also reflect the 'values' underpinning your organisation. Competence has two sides. The 'hard' side which relates to measurable outputs as well as a 'soft' side (which Woodruffe refers to as competen*cy* [2]) which describes the underpinning behavioural characteristics that make your organisation unique (e.g. ability of people to be 'friendly', 'self-assertive', etc.) Putting competence and competen*cy* together gives you a framework within which you can describe any job. What is more the *process* of describing jobs in this way will help you recognise *capability* within your organisation you never saw before. [3]

3.2 What's in it for me?

1. Once a job is defined in competence terms you can immediately use the result for selection, training and appraisal, and as a basis for reward management (see later chapters).

2. It enables you to see your organisation in terms of interlinked functions and not isolated roles. This hasimplications for the way people can work together in teams (*see* Chapter 9).

3. It provides a basis for putting a value on people in your organisation and rewarding success (*see* Chapter 8). If your company is approved to assess staff against specific NVQs (*see* section 3.3) you can give added value to staff by recommending them for NVQs in the marketplace.

4. It provides a route for development and career progression. By specifying competences required for every level of job in your organisation (including your own!) you make it clear to everyone what is required at higher levels. As a result everyone can then seek out the kind of opportunities to give them evidence of competence they need for career progression (*see* section 4 for how **Butlins Southcoast World** uses NVQs).

5. It reveals value in people which you may never before have realised they had.

3.3 What's involved?

First you need to redefine all occupational roles in terms of functions which can be separately identified and assessed. Below we take you through the breakdown of the job described in Figure 3.1 to explore how this job might be viewed differently if one took a 'competence' approach. We then look at how jobs/functions can be measured against NVQs.

Redefining jobs in terms of competences

Stage 1. What is the purpose of the job? (in this case Activity Assistant at the Oasis Leisure Centre). It is contained within statement (a) under **responsible for**. (Statement (b) is not an output but a means to an end which will be dealt with separately). We might state the purpose as follows:

> To **provide a service** which ensures **every customer** can **enjoy all the facilities** at the centre **safely, securely** and **without interference**.

The words used in the statement of purpose are critical because they define what is *unique* about the job. We have underlined what seems to be the critical phrases. Each of these become a main **functional** heading which will in turn be broken down until we arrive at a set of activities which are separately measurable — each of which by definition can be related back to the main purpose.

Stage 2. Separate out the key functions. In this case they relate to six areas:
1. Provision of service.
2. Service to be tailored to range of customers.

3. Ability to operate and be familiar with range of facilities/equipment.
4. Ensure safety of the customer.
5. Ensure the security of the customer.
6. Ensure customer enjoys facility without interference.

Stage 3. Taking each function in turn, ask the question: 'What needs to happen for this function to be achieved?' In Figure 3.2 each function area is broken down into a subset of specific activities that need to take place.

Provision of service	• Information • Technical help • Maintenance • Cleanliness • First Aid
Service tailored to customers	• Identify customer type • Match service to individual needs • Evaluate success • Train others • Explain range
Prepare range of facilities	• Set up equipment • Take equipment down
Ensure safe environment	• Follow safety regulations • Carry out safety audits • Identify/anticipate potential risks
Ensure secure environment	• Carry out security checks • Carry out evacuation procedure
Ensure customer enjoys facilities without interference	• Identify/anticipate potential causes of friction • Diffuse conflict in user friendly way

Figure 3.2 Breakdown of role of Activity Assistant

Stage 4. The competences described in Figure 3.2 by their very nature are 'general' — in fact that is the purpose behind the Government's aim to produce national standards that are *transferrable*. But the job description (Figure 3.1) specifies a range of specific contexts and situations within which the Activity Assistant would be expected to be competent. When we come to look at the format of NVQs below we will see this range of situations in which an employee has to demonstrate competence are called *range indicators*. Thus, to be competent as an Activity Assistant, an employee would need to demonstrate evidence of safety procedures not just in one section (pool side for instance) but in *all* areas identified in Figure 3.3.

Stage 5. Underpinning the range is a body of knowledge which is necessary to be proficient. This can be absorbed into the range or listed separately as we have done below.

Knowledge underpinning competences in Figures 3.2 and 3.3:

- First aid.
- Thamesdown operational procedures.
- Operation of equipment.
- Chemical agents for cleaning.

1. Range of Activity locations:
    - Dry changing rooms
    - Wet changing rooms
    - Leisure pool
    - Domebusters
    - Surrounding spectator areas
    - Pool hall
    - Glass areas
    - Roller skating
    - Showers and toilets
    - Control point into pool

2. Range of sports equipment.

3. Customer types:
    - Mums with toddlers
    - Families
    - Teenagers
    - Disabled
    - Learning difficulties
    - Elderly

4. Range of supplies:
    - Chemicals
    - Cleaning equipment

Figure 3.3 Range indicators

Industry lead body	General title	Level
Sports & recreation	Sport & recreation	1
	Facility operations	2
Mrs Judi Stock, Local Government Management Board,	Coaching & activity delivery (adults/ children/disabled)	2, 3
Armdale House	Playwork	2, 3
Armdale Centre	Supervision	3
Luton LU1 2TS	Outdoor education	3
Tel 0582 451166	Sports development	3, 4
	Playwork development	4
	Facility management	4
Amenity Horticulture	Amenity horticulture Nursery — Interior	1
Mr John Conway (Address as above)	Soft landscape maintenance	2
	Greenkeeping/sports Turf, sports grounds maintenance	2
	Arboriculture	2
	Hard landscaping	2
Hotel & Catering Dr Anne Walker Hotel & Catering Training Company, International House High St Ealing W5 5DB 081 579 2400	Wide range of NVQs accredited — see Figure 3.6 for examples	2,3,4,5

Other Lead Bodies developing standards relevant to the Leisure Industry are:
- Museum Training Institute (0274 391092).
- Agricultural Training Board (0203 696996).
- Arts & Entertainment Training council (0532 448845).

Contact ILAM for further details.

Figure 3.4 Some of the N/SVQs available appropriate to the leisure industry

The NVQ framework

In 1986 the Government established the National Council for Vocational Qualifications (NCVQ) to oversee the development and approval of national occupational standards. The standards themselves are devised by what are called Industry Lead Bodies in consultation with employers in a particular industry. There are no less than nine Industry Lead Bodies that cover standards for the leisure industry. These include sport and recreation, hotel and catering, amenity horticulture, etc. Figure 3.4 presents an extract from an ILAM Briefing sheet of just some of the N/SVQs appropriate to the industry together with details of respective Lead Bodies.

The Industry Lead Bodies develop the standards but are not necessarily responsible for their award. This is down to awarding bodies like City and Guilds and BTEC, who are approved by NCVQ to award specific NVQs on the basis of assessment carried out in the company or other approved agency. If you wish to introduce relevant NVQs (or the equivalent SVQ if you are in Scotland) into your organisation you would need to be approved by the appropriate awarding body.

On the other hand you might choose to use the standards published by the Industry Lead Bodies to develop standards for your own company. Instead of having to break down a job description in the way we have done above you will find the analysis has already been carried out for you and all the details provided in the format in which all NVQs are presented.

In Figure 3.5 is an example of an NVQ *unit* from the Hotel and Catering Lead Body, the Hotel and Catering Training Company. This unit is concerned with maintaining a secure environment which is common to a number of functions. A unit is made up of a collection of activities called *elements*. By demonstrating that you can meet specific criteria appropriate to each element that make up a unit you can get a record of achievement for that unit. As soon as you receive credits for all units covered by an NVQ you are awarded an NVQ at a particular level.

The criteria you need to satisfy are of two kinds — *performance criteria* and *range indicators* (*see* Figure 3.5). Performance indicators are the criteria an assessor uses to ask themselves 'what evidence is there that that employee has met their performance criterion?'. The range indicators indicate the variety of situations within which an employee would need to demonstrate the performance criteria. For example, if you were assessing a pool attendant's competence at being able to spot signs that a bather is in difficulty — you may want to test this competence in different situations — when pool is full, half full, near empty, etc.

If you are new to these concepts don't be put off by the jargon. It may seem all very theoretical but there are very practical benefits to be had from thinking about the various roles in your organisation in competence terms using the format described in Figure 3.5. In the section below you can see how **Butlins Southcoast World** has comprehensively introduced NVQs throughout the organisation and the benefits that have accrued as a result.

3.4 Examples of good practice

The job description in Figure 3.1 is from the **Oasis Leisure Centre**. Job descriptions still tend to be the norm among our case studies but **Butlins Southcoast World** is currently reviewing whether it needs 132 different job descriptions.

MOMI has done much to create a new role, that of 'first-person interpreter'. It has a very clear picture of the *effect* the 'interpreter' has to bring about: to 'enliven and enhance' a particular period in the history of the cinema. It defines the job in a single paragraph without the need of a detailed job description:

Catering and Hospitality Industry and Licensed Trade: Occupational Standards for NVQs/SVQs Level 2

Key Roles	A/C/D	Core Unit
Unit	G1	Maintain a Safe and Secure Working Environment
Element	G1.5	Maintain a Secure Environment for Customers, Staff and Visitors

Performance Criteria

1) Establishment property is secured in accordance with laid down procedures.
2) Customer, staff and storage areas are secured against unauthorised access.
3) Keys are secured from unauthorised access at all times.
4) Missing establishment, staff or customer property is reported to the appropriate person.
5) Suspicious individuals are politely challenged or reported in accordance with laid down procedures.
6) Lost property is dealt with in accordance with laid down procedures.

Range

Staff areas:
* work areas
* staff facilities

Storage areas:
* store rooms and cellars
* store cupboards and cabinets
* fridges and freezers

Lost property:
* not suspicious items or packages

Customer areas:
* private facilities for customers
* public areas

Laid down procedures:
* all relevant health and safety legislation
* all relevant establishment procedures

Catering and Hospitality Industry and Licensed Trade: Occupational Standards for NVQs/SVQs Level 2

Key Roles	A/C/D	Core Unit
Unit	G1	Maintain a Safe and Secure Working Environment
Element	G1.5	Maintain a Secure Environment for Customers, Staff and Visitors

Underpinning Knowledge Evidence:

- why keys, property and areas should be secured from unauthorised access at all times.

Assessment Methods

Evidence of competence to cover all of the performance criteria across the range must be assessed using one of the following methods:

A) Totally by observation in the workplace or realistic work environment.

B) Observation for a minimum of:

  i) 1 from the range of staff areas
  ii) 1 from the range of storage areas
  iii) 1 from the range of customer areas

Plus supplementary evidence in the form of:

a) Questioning which can be oral using visual aids or technology based aids.
b) Simulations in the workplace or realistic work environment.

Evidence of underpinning knowledge must be assessed by questioning, which can be oral using visual aids or technology based aids.

Figure 3.5 Example of an NVQ unit from the Hotel and Catering Training Company Reproduced with their kind permission.

> *Actors in MOMI are first-person interpreters who work on their own in two areas on alternate weeks. They research the social and film history of the two areas using prepared research material, books, film and video and attending seminars. Once cast, actors devise their own characters working in small groups with the director. These characters will interact with the public, give information, entertain, demonstrate exhibits and commentate on films.*

It is interesting that in this case it is the *context* within which the role will literally be played out that defines the job. Recruiting for acting skills is not enough. If the job were to be defined in competence terms it would be the range indicators which would provide the clue to what makes for a successful interpreter. These might be some of the underlying 'competencies':

- listening skills
- improvisation skills
- energy
- ability to relate to range of public (small children, foreign tourists, disabled) and adopt an appropriate script
- visualisation skills
- ability to learn very quickly
- maintain equilibrium under pressure
- self-awareness.

Though an actor would have many of these skills the *context* of interacting with the public and improvising within the boundaries of a self-imposed time-warp is very different from being centre stage and delivering a set-script. As we shall see in Chapters 4 and 5 this has implications for how **MOMI** goes about recruiting and selecting staff.

Butlins Southcoast World is a very good example of a company that has enthusiastically taken on board NVQs to such an extent that it has been approved by a number of Awarding Bodies not only to assess its own staff against NVQs but also to train assessors of other companies. The Personnel and Training Executive talks now of a 'culture of NVQs'. But it was very different when he joined in December 1989. There was a need to change the culture and improve levels of professionalism and commitment of the staff. The clue for how this could be done came out of early work with the Hotel and Catering Training Board, who pioneered a competence-based approach to accreditation of catering staff — the scheme was called 'Caterbase'. **Butlins Southcoast World** used the scheme to set standards for its cooks, waitresses and bar staff.

However, it was soon realised that a 'competence-based' approach could only have an impact on the business if it embraced *all* occupations, *including* management. By this time other NVQs were coming on stream. So he began to identify NVQs that were relevant to other occupations. Figure 3.6 summarises the range of NVQs currently offered to staff.

The support and administration of such a scheme itself requires the development of further skills — notably those of assessors. **Butlins Southcoast World's** aim is to have every supervisor accredited as an NVQ assessor, for which specific standards have been set by the Training and Development Lead Body (TDLB). The company has established a separate profit centre to train assessors in other organisations. In addition the local TEC sends trainees to **Butlins Southcoast World** to be trained to NVQ standards. The funding for these trainees pays for the NVQ accreditation of **Butlins Southcoast World's** own staff.

A key factor in **Butlins Southcoast World's** successful introduction of NVQs is that they are an *integral* part of the company's development strategy for all staff which is called the 'Stars' programme. (This is described in Chapter 6.) Stars are awarded to all new starters after

Currently Butlins offers NVQs to employees in the following occupations:	They are awarded through the following bodies:
• Reception • Portering • F&B service/bars • F&B service/restaurant • Food preparation & cooking • Serving food and drink • Housekeeping • Retail • Security guarding • Child care and education • Building cleaning (Interiors) • Business administration • Admininstration & finance • Training & development • Training assessor & verifier • Quality service • Amenity horticulture	• Hotel & Catering Training Company (HCTC) • Sports and Recreation Board * City and Guilds

Figure 3.6 NVQs at Southcoast World

successful completion of critical stages of the development programme. The highest award is 'Five Star' which is dependent on an employee successfully completing an appropriate NVQ at level 2.

One consequence of raising the skill level of the workforce through NVQs is that it improves the capability of each department to meet the needs of the customers; this can lead to restructuring and reorganisation. After six staff of a bar in **Butlins Southcoast World** had achieved NVQ level 2 it was found that working practices had improved to the extent that service standards could be maintained with just four staff. This meant that the skills of the other two could be used to 'add value' to service in another bar.

Butlins Southcoast World recognises that the reward it gains from investment in NVQs is a growing bank of skills which canbe used in flexible ways to meet the changing needs of the market. An NVQ level 2 is fast becoming the basic skill requirement for all jobs — which is also the benchmark in recruitment ads. Increasingly they will use their own skillbase to fill internal positions at all levels from within the company. **Butlins Southcoast World** is well on the way to contributing to the Government's national target that by 1996 50 per cent of the workforce should be working towards NVQs.

3.5 Lessons to be learned

1. The way jobs are defined says a lot about the culture of the organisation. But, as we saw in Chapter 1, as the culture is always changing so are jobs — does the way jobs are currently defined do justice to your current organisation?

2. If you have a clear vision about how the job should be undertaken — *see* **MOMI**, section 3.4 — that should influence the way it is described. If you haven't you may find that

carrying out the kind of 'functional analysis' we have described helps you see roles, jobs you have taken for granted in a different way. It may reveal added value you hadn't seen before; it may reveal gaps which need to be filled; it may have implications for grouping/restructuring.

3. The way you define individual roles in your organisation has to be specific enough to attract appropriate skills (*see* Chapter 4) and for staff to be clear about individual accountability; but roles must also be capable of growing and adding value to the organisation as a whole. This is a theme to which we will continually return.

4. One way of adding value is through matching your occupational roles with NVQs. NVQs can be used as the basis for a company-wide development programme which gives individuals value in the market place.

3.6 Action plan

1. Starting with the purpose/mission statement you produced (*see* Chapter 1) break this down into no more than four or five key functions that have to be achieved for the mission to be realised.

2. Taking each function in turn ask yourself what has to happen for this function to be achieved, and break down into subsets until you arrive at a manageable set of activities. These are the core competences. You may be surprised that these are not as specialised as are tasks of a job description. The advantage is that the process frees you from looking at jobs within rigid boundaries — as a result you are better able to see connections *between* functions. It also means that you can recognise opportunities for internal changes, appointments.

3. If you already have job descriptions see if you can match them with the competences arrived at above. You can also carry out the same exercise on each one as we carried out with the job description from **Oasis Leisure Centre**.

4. Find a format for describing the job that suits you and your organisation. Figures 3.1, 3.2 and 3.3 may give you some ideas; they also share the same framework as the national occupational standards, NVQs (*see* Figure 3.5). On the other hand you may have to follow a format appropriate to local authority procedure, for example (as in Figure 3.1). But the words you use to describe jobs and roles can still open up rather than close down opportunities for staff.

Additional, or complementary, actions are to:

5. Match competences from the above analysis or range of occupations/functions performed with NVQs currently available (*see* list in Figure 3.4).

6. Re-write existing functions within competence framework using existing NVQs if available.

7. Identify member/s of staff who can act as mentors/assessors or be trained as assessors. If you wish to be approved as an NVQ centre you will be required to train assessors up to TDLB standards D32 and/or D33.

8. Test out validity of a competence profile for a particular occupation:
    — As an aid to recruitment (*see* Chapter 4): does it identify particular characteristics, skills which can help target your recruitment campaign?
    — As an aid to selection (*see* Chapter 5) does it help you create an exercise/test-case which requires the applicant to demonstrate particular characteristics critical to job success?
    — As the basis for training/development of:
      • New staff: does it provide new starters with a list of competences and outline of resources they can draw on to help them achieve them? (*see* Chapter 6).
      • Existing staff: can it be used as the basis of an appraisal scheme? (*see* Chapter 7))

9. Evaluate in terms of added-value (*see* Chapter 8).

10. Plan how to introduce to other occupations and consider the implications for support resources needed.

3.7 References

1. Training Agency (1989) *Development of Assessable Standards for National Certification* — Guidance Note 2, Employment Department, Moorfoot.

2. Woodruffe, C. (1991) Competent by any other name *Personnel Management* September 1991, pp. 30–33.

3. Critten, P. (1993) *Investing in People: Towards Corporate Capability* Butterworth Heinemann.

4. Jessup, G. (1991) *Outcomes: NVQs and the emerging model of Education and Training* Falmer Press.

4. A targeted approach to recruitment

4.1 The principles

> *Overall, an HRM approach to recruitment involves taking much more care in matching people to the requirements of the organisation as a whole, as well as to the particular needs of the job.*[1]

> *The HRM approach to resourcing...emphasises that matching resources to organisational requirements does not simply mean maintaining the status quo and perpetuating a moribund culture. It can, and often does, mean radical changes in thinking about the competences required in the future to achieve sustainable growth and cultural change.*[1]

These two quotes give a flavour of an HRM approach to recruitment which follows on from Chapter 3 whose theme was opening up descriptions of jobs to reveal underlying and interlinking organisational value.

We have to face the same dilemma here as in Chapter 3: on the one hand you have to be as specific as you can to *target* the kind of people you want to do a specific job now, but you also want to lay a foundation for growth which may require a greater *diversity* and mix of skills than you have at present.

You also have to be aware of the legal rights of *potential* employees (*see* Chapter 2). In particular whatever methods you use to recruit staff must comply with Equal Opportunity rights — i.e. you must not be seen to discriminate against people on grounds of race, sex, age and disabilities. On the other hand you *do* have the right to *positively discriminate* in favour of applications from groups who have been underrepresented in the workforce in previous 12 months (e.g. women, ethnic minorities).

Rank Xerox wanted to change perception of local people in Milton Keynes (an area traditionally of low unemployment) that the job of 'Customer Response Controller' was a woman's role. With the approval of the Equal Opportunities Commission it ran an advertising campaign with the theme: 'Why are good men so difficult to find?' Not only did it receive more applications from men than before but they *also* received more applications from women and were able to recruit four men and five women.[2]

This is a good example of 'targeted' recruitment whereby a *specific* message is likely to attract not only a particular group (in this case men) but also tends to raise the overall standards of *all* applicants as Rank Xerox found. At a time of recession and high unemployment this is particularly important as companies find themselves inundated with so many applications for one advertised job.

With a predicted decline in number of school leavers, target recruitment is also a response by a company to attracting its share of the increasing growing sector of the labour market — women, ethnic minorities, mature adults. But if you are seeking to diversify your workforce you must convince your target group that 'they can see evidence that people like themselves are already successfully employed by the organisation or at the very least made welcome by it'[3] — otherwise 'they' won't apply.

The way you do this is the subject of the section.4.3

4.2 What's in it for me?

1. If you know where you want to 'target' recruitment can help you get there. Remember you can also use the same approach for *internal* appointments though internal candidates might need more convincing (after all they will *know* the present incumbents!).

2. It is cost effective. The better you target your recruitment campaign the more self-selective potential applicants will be. A number of years ago one of the national brewers got tired of explaining to hopeful managers that it was unlikely they would get a pub of their dreams — in the country, with retirement days happily spent chatting to the locals. They therefore ran an advertising campaign (on TV and in newspapers) which depicted a manager on the end of a broken bottle in an inner-city pub. The punch line was that if they could cope with a situation like this they just *might* be what the brewer was looking for. There was significant time saved processing unsuitable applications and it resulted in a better standard of couples applying.

4.3 What's involved?

As was suggested at the beginning of this chapter an HRM approach to recruitment is more concerned with thinking about future staff in the context of the organisation as a whole and not in any one particular job. In fact even if you have no vacancy at present we recommend the activities outlined in the Action Plan as an exercise in *visualising* the kind of people your organisation needs to employ to realise the mission, vision and values you arrived at in the Action Plan at the end of Chapter 1.

The start and end point is with a clear picture of the organisation you wish to become. This enables you to draw up a profile of the *typical* employee whose characteristics will help you realise your mission. You then use this picture to attract a *particular* type of person, through an advert in the local paper or through a brochure.

An IPM survey of 1,000 personnel professionals carried out in 1989 indicated that by far the most popular method of recruitment was through advertisements in the press.[3] Eighty-seven per cent used regional press, 80 per cent specialist press and 78 per cent national press. Adverts need to include information on five topics:[4]

- the organisation
- the job
- selection criteria
- salary and benefits
- how to apply.

However, depending on the nature of the job, organisations may not reveal details of the salary, preferring to 'negotiate' a 'reward management package' (*see* Chapter 8). In the examples given in this chapter there is no information about salary.

The aim of this chapter is not to make you an expert in writing copy for job adverts (*see* Fowler (1990) and Plumbley (1985) for more detailed help), but to help you be clear about the *message* you need to convey regardless of the media you choose to use.

As we shall see in section 4.4 a number of our case studies preferred to use another method — that of open days — which has distinct advantages for enabling potential staff to experience the working conditions for themselves. In the leisure industry it is the *context* within which work takes place that is often the key.

Prior to 1988 the water theme park, **Thorpe Park**, in Surrey had tended to depend on agency staff until it realised just how costly it was and, worst of all, that it led to reduced performance standards and consequent visitor dissatisfaction. In 1988 it carried out a review of its staffing procedures and identified two key problems:

1. The Park was perceived by local people to be a poor employer offering mundane service jobs with low staff morale.

2. Poor induction training amongst new starters led to high turnover within the first two weeks.

To tackle the first problem it launched an open day in February just prior to its opening to the public. In 1991 this attracted almost a thousand hopeful applicants who were able to visit the attractions for themselves and personally talk through their application with friendly staff.

As **Beaulieu** and **Butlins Southcoast World** report below, the staff attracted through these open days may only be contracted for a season but many return year after year ensuring the organisations have a ready trained pool of staff to draw on.

4.4 Examples of good practice

Beaulieu

The Personnel Manager, Jan Hoy, organises six to eight open days a year which she prefers to call 'induction days'. Her rationale is that even if a person is not recruited they will never forget the '**Beaulieu** experience'. It is organised in a fun way (Figure 4.1 depicts the day as a journey/race).

During the course of the day each applicant will have:

- talked about themselves (for one minute which is tape-recorded)
- toured the attractions
- seen a film on **Beaulieu**
- worked on a group project
- completed individual numeracy and verbal tests.

On top of all this the Personnel Manager will have made time to talk personally to everyone (average number 30-40).

At the end of the day **Beaulieu** cannot guarantee a job. For one thing Jan Hoy admits that she hasn't a clear idea of type or number of jobs (because employees from previous years will often return for another season). But what she ensures is that when she needs them she can draw on a wide range of personalities and skills which she will keep on record. Expensive it may be but it reflects the professional way the organisation invests in its staff even before they join.

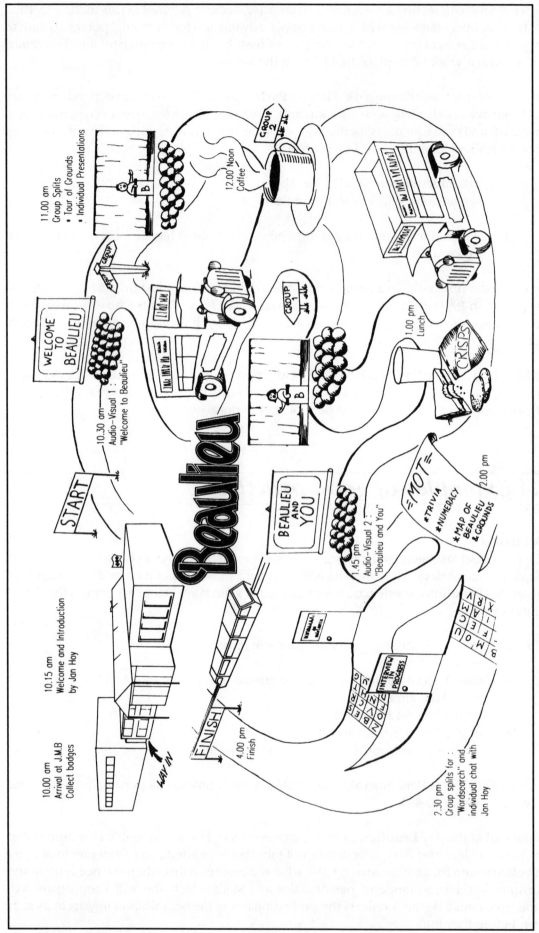

Figure 4.1 Plan of Beaulieu's induction day for staff recruitment

MOMI

Three times a year the Company Manager holds an audition in response to an advert (*see* Figure 4.2) which is usually placed in the actors' magazine, *Stage*. This will usually attract about 200 people of whom 100 are auditioned for just 18 parts.

Figure 4.2 MOMI's staff recruitment advert

The Company Manager and Director run the day's event during the course of which 100 will be reduced to 18. This is done by a series of games and improvisation exercises at which both the Director and Manager are looking for qualities needed by an 'interpreter', viz:

- improvisation skills
- energy
- eye contact with audience
- voice quality
- listening skills.

In addition, because of the amount of study required to get inside their period, they will often look to actors who also have a degree.

4.5 Lessons to be learned

1. The above organisations are very clear about the kind of person they want to employ who is *right for the organisation* though they may not be able to say exactly what role

that person may play. This is in contrast to a traditional approach to recruitment where a person is recruited for a specific position. The leisure industry may indeed be in advance of tradition in recruiting on the basis of more generic skills, competences which can be used in flexible ways.

2. The value of the open day is in involving applicants directly within the context and culture of the organisation. It gives them an opportunity to find out if they are comfortable in that environment. (At **MOMI** auditions a proportion of actors withdraw themselves because they realise the role is not for them.) At the same time it enables the organisation to assess the individual in the real work environment. In this sense it comes closer to the notion of an 'assessment centre', which we will look at in the next chapter.

4.6 Action plan

1. Start with your mission. Look at what you have written in your Action Plan following Chapter 1. Write down in your Action Plan the *kind* of staff who would most reflect these values.

   For example, look at the mission of a hypothetical Leisure pool we discussed in Chapter 1:

   > *All our staff have a dual commitment to the community (especially the disabled) and to helping as many people from the community experience and enjoy our facilities to the full.*

   Added to the values described in Chapter 1 (being friendly/enjoying the facilities) the 'typical' member of staff might have the following characteristics:
   — be from the local community
   — have experience of working with disabled
   — have strong interest in /experience of sport.

2. Now review the kind of employment contract that best works for your kind of business and the legal implications — *see* the Action Plan following Chapter 2. What are the implications for a change in recruitment policy — higher proportion of women, ethnic minorities, disabled, over 50s? What are implications for more flexible working arrangements which can be offered — to mothers with young children for example? *How* are people expected to work together — under close supervision or as autonomous teams? (*see* Chapter 9).

3. You must also take account of the mix of competences you need in response to the kind of functional analysis you carried out in Chapter 3. For example, a functional analysis of our hypothetical leisure pool's requirements, in point one, might reveal the need for all staff to have a much more detailed knowledge of and expertise in all aspects of health and fitness.

4. If you take account of all these factors you are in a position to 'target' recruitment more effectively. In your Action Plan devise a recruitment advertisement for a new member of staff. At this stage don't be over concerned about what to call them. Take the view that in the future to achieve the purpose you have defined you will need staff that meet the following requirements: … Take it from there.

   Figure 4.3 shows an example of a 'targeted' advert for our hypothetical leisure centre (called the Ajax Leisure Centre) which identifies the kind of person needed as well as describing the kind of 'team' environment in which the person will be expected to demonstrate competence.

A targeted approach to recruitment is a cost-effective way of improving the calibre of applicants. But before offering a contract of employment you will need to carefully SELECT those who most closely match your requirements. This is the subject of the next chapter.

Are you mad about swimming and fitness? Would you like to help others — especially the disabled — help themselves to be fitter?

If so, you might be just the person we are looking for at the Ajax Leisure Centre to join our team of fitness professionals. At Ajax we want to encourage more of the Afro-Caribbean community to enjoy our facilities.

If you are from this community and particularly if you have experience of dealing with the disabled we want to hear from you. Equally we want to hear from anyone who believes they have something to offer us.

You must, of course, be able to swim. It would also be desirable for you to have the Bronze medallion in life saving. But we don't expect anything else other than a real commitment to fitness through water-related activities. We are also looking for people who have exciting new ideas for encouraging the disabled to take up our facilities.

We work as a team so that in any one week you are likely to be assisting in all areas of the pool — including gym and sauna. We also encourage all staff to gain National Vocational Qualifications (NVQs) in all aspects of leisure and leisure management.

If you have something to offer us and believe we can help your career, let's talk some more. Contact....

Figure 4.3 Example of a 'targeted' advert

4.7 References

1. Armstrong, M. (1992) *Human Resource Management — Strategy and Action* Kogan Page, p. 139 and p. 136.

2. Paddison, L. (1990) The targeted approach to recruitment *Personnel Management* November 1990, pp. 54–58.

3. Curnow, B. (1989) Recruit, retrain, retain: personnel management and the three Rs *Personnel Management* November 1990, pp. 40–47.

4. Fowler, A. (1990) How to write a job advertisement *Personnel Management Plus* Vol. 1, No. 4, October 1990 pp. 31–32.

5. Plumbley, P. (1985) *Recruitment and Selection* IPM.

5. Opening up selection

1. The principles

The strategy for the 1990s makes selection methods more important than ever. It is not their usefulness which is in question but how they are used. Some of them (job sample exercises, situational interviews, biographphic data, tests of aptitude, assessment centres) are the most reliable and valid sources of information that we have about applicants' suitability. But if both parties are taking decisions, both need the benefit of such information. It is how these instruments are incorporated into the design of the recruitment and selection procedure that matters. One thing is for sure — the procedure can no longer be designed as if it is organisations which are the only ones doing the selecting.[1]

Consider this first of two scenarios. You have applied for a job which attracts you (we assume the company has practised 'targeted recruitment'). You ring the contact number and are immediately invited for an interview. The interviewer hardly asks you any questions at all and after ten minutes you are offered the job.

Now consider the second scenario. Again a job advert attracts your attention and you ring a contact number. You are asked for your address and next day you receive an application form. You look at the three pages you are required to fill in with some trepidation but after a while you begin to feel encouraged because you are enabled to present information about yourself which you'd quite forgotten. You send off the application form and names of two referees. The procedure is then as follows:

1. About a week later you receive a card acknowledging receipt of your application form and advising you that the company will contact you in due course.

2. After another week you receive a letter informing you that you have been short-listed for the job and inviting you to attend not just an interview but a one-day event which includes: short introduction to job; individual exercises; group activity; individual interview.

3. On the day you are first introduced to five other people who you realise are the five others short-listed with you for the job! But over coffee as you get to know the others you quite forget you've come here for an interview. As a group you are addressed by the Company Director who then hands over to the Personnel Manager who introduces a 15-minute video on the company and then spends another ten minutes introducing the job in the context of what you've seen in the video. The session ends with questions and answers.

4. The six of you are then ushered into separate rooms. It is explained to you what the company is looking for in the job and in particular the key competences required. What it would like you to do is to complete two psychometric tests (one is a personality test and the other a test of numeracy) and then write a report in response to how you would market a new facility that is being introduced. This takes up about an hour. You are told that you will be given feedback on the two psychometric tests.

5. You then join the five others who have been through the same process and as a group are required to share the proposals you each made in your marketing reports and as a group decide on best approach or agree a new strategy. You have 45 minutes to come to this decision. You notice that the person who tested you along with five others are taking notes. At the end it is explained that in the afternoon each of you will be having a 20-minute interview. It is up to you to agree which of you will be interviewed when.

6. You then have lunch as a group and are joined by the company managers and all people involved in the morning's events.

7. After lunch and before your interview you are given feedback on how you did on the psychometric tests. You are pleasantly surprised to see that your profile corresponds to your own self-perception but a bit disappointed in the results from the numeracy test. But the person who administered the test reassures you. You are then given a guided tour of the buildings and meet managers who would be your colleagues. You notice how open they are about giving you any information you require.

8. At the interview you are first asked to give your impressions about the day, about the company and to put any questions you may have. The manager then takes you through your application form encouraging you to expand on what you have achieved in the past and finally asking why you want the job and what you think you can contribute to it. In conclusion you are told the company will be contacting you within the next two days.

9. Two days later you receive a letter regretting that the company is not going to offer you the job. But it is not a standard letter because it goes on to congratulate you on your response to the marketing exercise and identifies ideas you remember you came up with. Finally it confirms that the company would like to keep your application and notes on file for future positions if you have no objection. You are also cordially invited to contact the company if you would like to ask anything further.

Accepting that the second is very much an ideal scenario and that the cost of a company going to all this trouble would probably be prohibitive, the point it makes is the *principle* underpinning this illustration which is summarised in the opening quotation.

What would be your reaction to the job offer from the first scenario? It would depend no doubt on how desperate you were for the job! But you would probably have some questions about why the company is so desperate to take you without really finding out anything about you. What is more you were not able to find out much about them.

The second scenario is as detailed as it is because we want to pick up many of the points raised later in the chapter. Your reaction to it might be that if this was you you'd be annoyed at having wasted a day of your time. On the other hand you might take the view that the day was more like a training course than a selection event and that you've learned not just about the company (which must have gone up in your estimation) but about yourself.

Of course, economics would mean that the kind of arrangements made in the second scenario would be likely to apply only to very senior management jobs. But the *principle* it illustrates is that the selection process can reflect very powerfully the company culture to the extent that thought should be given to what aspects of scenario two could apply to the selection of *anyone* in your organisation. We will examine the process in section 4.3, but first we consider this proposition from Peter Heriot who is quoted at the beginning of the chapter:

> *The procedure for the 1990s requires organisations to treat the applicant as being on an equal footing with themselves to share all the information available and to surrender some of the power that they hold simply because they are in charge of the procedure.*[1]

The concept of 'empowerment' will come up later in the book but it is interesting at this stage to speculate that it starts at selection. An organisation that shows themselves to be completely open and clear what they want at the time of selection and invites you to be as honest with them *must* have an empowering culture.

5.2 What's in it for me?

1. The *way* you go about selecting staff sends out a signal about the way you are likely to value those staff once they join. Any company that went to the trouble outlined in scenario two *must* value its staff. The trick though is that there ought to be a similar *principle* applied to the selection of any member of staff not just the high fliers. Peter Heriot[1] also suggests that many applicants are heavily influenced to accept the job offer or not according to the way they were treated at selection.

2. The selection process should be accessible and *communicated* to all members of staff because it literally adds value to a particular job or set of skills. By definition, the amount of trouble the company is prepared to go to in order to fill a particular role indicates its value for the *internal* as well as the external market.

3. Having gone to the trouble you have in the previous chapter to target recruitment so that you attract the best possible candidates in the most cost-effective way the selection process must be that more sensitive to identify the best of the best, otherwise you are not capitalising on your investment.

4. HRM literally sees people as assets; selection followed by a job offer involves a high cost. You must take every step you can to ensure that assets are going to be productive as soon as possible and to involve minimum costs. Training is often seen as a cost (*see* Chapter 6) but you will note that a comprehensive selection process could be seen as the *beginning* of the training process.

5.3 What's involved?

Before you can start the selection process you must have clearly defined the specific competences required. You needed this at the last stage, recruitment, but you might have had only a broad picture of the profile of the person you needed. At selection you must arrive at very specific criteria otherwise you will spend time developing procedures which are assessing the wrong criteria.

A company wanted to select sales executives and assumed that a key quality was 'sociability'. It therefore set about designing exercises which would test for this competency. 'Later research showed this factor was irrelevant to sales success and that what should have been tested were qualities of independence and persistence.'[2]

Before proceeding further check back to what you have described in your Action Plan after Chapter 4.

The object of the selection process is to progressively reduce the number of applicants you have attracted through your recruitment campaign until you have a short-list of applicants whom you can assess in a more intensive way to arrive at the most suitable candidate. The number of reductions depends on the number of applicants and the nature of the position to be filled. But generally there are just two stages.

Stage 1: Selection on paper

Even if there are a small number of applications, many companies require all candidates to complete a company application form because even if a candidate isn't successful their records can be kept on file in case a future vacancy occurs. If you have thousands of applications the application form is your opportunity to screen out less suitable candidates. It is crucial therefore that the application form gives you information on which you can make these decisions.

There is enormous scope to create attractive application forms which pose the minimum of questions to derive the maximum of information. Some companies prefer the candidates not to fill in standard forms, leaving them free to make an individual presentation. But it is impossible to quickly process unstandardised applications.

What you need is a very simple break-down into key areas which also gives qualitative data to build up a profile in your own mind of this candidate who you might never meet.Equally, if they are short-listed, the form will be the basis for the interview with the candidate at which you will want to focus on key areas to explore further. An example breakdown might be:

- Personal details (lately there have been suggestions that 'bio' data (biographical) could correlate with success in certain positions).
- Past employment details supported by examples of what the applicant considered was their greatest achievement.
- Education, training and qualifications.
- Outside interests, again supported by examples of achievement. (As we shall see later there is a tendency to overlook competences a person has achieved outside a purely vocational area. Clearly membership of St John's Ambulance or being secretary of a community social club could have important implications for a job in leisure.)
- Opportunity to summarise what kind of contribution they feel they could make in the job role.
- Aspirations for the future: this might prove a useful basis for discriminating between applicants on the basis of their vision for the future.
- Referees.

On the basis of applications received you now have to draw up a short-list of six to eight candidates who *on paper* meet your requirements.

But what are your requirements?

In order to devise the recruitment advert you produced in your Action Plan in Chapter 4 you had to take account of the Mission for your company, the particular labour market you intended to tap and the kind of competences that make up the job/role. By and large this was a 'macro' view — you want to recruit a person that fits into the company culture. When it comes to selection you need to take more of a 'micro' view — getting into more detail about the specific competences that are required (*see* Chapter 3). In that chapter we made a distinction between competence and competency — the former being an occupational standard and the latter to do with underlying behavioural characteristics. When it comes to selection we need to bring these both together.

Traditionally they have come together in what is called a 'person specification' which is usually based on a 7-point plan devised by an English occupational psychologist, Alec Rodger in the 1950s.[3] Figure 5.1 summarises the seven critical characteristics that Rodger claimed could be used to compare one job applicant with another.

1.	Physical make-up	health, appearance, physique, etc.
2.	Attainments	education, qualifications, experience
3.	General intelligence	verbal and numerical reasoning
4.	Special aptitudes	mechanical, spatial, verbal skills
5.	Interests	artistic, social, practical
6.	Disposition	acceptability, influence over others
7.	Circumstances	domestic arrangements, family

Alec Rodger's 7-point scale

Figure 5.2 is an example of a person specification for an Activities Assistant at the **Oasis Leisure Centre**. Notice that in Figure 5.2 some of the characteristics are subcategorised as being 'essential' or just 'desirable'.

Given that the person specification headings should correspond with headings on your application form it makes it more manageable to identify ideal candidates if you are faced with a deluge of applicants. Depending on what are considered absolutely essential qualities (e.g. qualifications and experience) you should be able to eliminate a number of applicants who *on paper* do not meet the minimum criteria.

However, as you will know if you've filled out such forms in the past, it is often the case that you don't always include all the information you could or necessarily present yourself in the best light. It may also be that some applicants will include *additional* information which persuade you that they are worth seeing although on paper they *don't* meet your minimum requirements. The application form should always give candidates the opportunity to surprise you!

Stage 2: Face-to-face selection

At the same time as you give the good news to the six to eight applicants selected for face-to-face interview and further assessment, you *must* inform the others that they have not met

POST TITLE: Full-time Activities Assistant

FOR INTERVIEW USE ONLY

Weighting (W) =
Candidate 6 5 4 3 2 1

1. **QUALIFICATIONS**
   Essential
   — RLSS Pool Lifeguard (or ability to pass)
   — GCSE English   x (w)=
   — First Aid Certificate (or ability to pass)   x (w)=
   Desirable   x (w)=
   — Advanced resuscitation   x (w)=
   — Relevant Sports Coaching certificate   x (w)=

2. **EXPERIENCE (relevant paid or unpaid)**
   Essential
   — Interest in sports related activities
   Desirable
   — Previous experience of work in a leisure/
     sports centre
   — Voluntary participation in a sports
     organisation
   — Some administrative experience

3. **TRAINING (relevant training previously
   received)**
   — Pool Plant Operation training/experience

4. **SKILLS**
   — Must be able to communicate effectively
     and adopt a leadership role
   — Must be able to work in a team
     environment and mix well] with the
     general public

5. **PERSONAL QUALITIES**
   — Lively and enthusiastic
   — Willing to learn new skills
   — Ability to work under pressure/act calmly
     in an emergency

6. **PRACTICAL ATTRIBUTES (special
   requirements such as lifting weights)**
   — Physically capable of carrying out the
     duties of the job description

7. **SEX (if genuine occupational qualification)**

8. **PREFERRED AGE RANGE**
   — 18+

INTERVIEW USE ONLY

CANDIDATE   TOTAL   ANY OTHER COMMENTS

ASSESSED BY   DESIGNATION

DATE

Figure 5.2 Example of person specification as used at Oasis Leisure Centre

the essential criteria. If they were to challenge this you are in a position to respond given the selection process carried out to-date.

The next stage is to plan just *how* you are going to discriminate between the six to eight applicants to select just one. (Of course you may end up with two who you can't choose between and require a further selection stage.)

There are a wide range of methods and techniques you can use. The most popular and widely used is the one-to-one interview, despite the fact that the British Psychological Society claims that the predictive validity coefficient of interviews is only 0.25 (in other words even well conducted interviews are only 25 per cent better than sticking a pin in a list of candidates).

But despite the interview's reputation for bias and discrimination it retains its popularity for psychological reasons, i.e. it affords a two-way exchange of views which isn't always possible through other methods we will examine. Before doing so it should be stressed that the 0.25 score afforded by the British Psychological Society only applied to *planned and structured* interviews. Unplanned interviews had zero predictive value!

For guidance on conducting an interview see Fowler (1991) and Courtis (1988) references. Here we would just emphasise three key aspects:

1. Preparation: before you see an applicant you should have analysed their application form (or CV) and identified key areas you would like to probe into more

2. Question technique: use open questions as much as possible (e.g. Why? How?) to give the applicant a maximum opportunity to respond and reveal information not covered on paper.

3. Timing and sequence: every applicant should get the same amount of time and the interview should follow the same pattern. Usually the application form is the basis on which the interviewer asks questions. At the end it is important that each applicant be given the opportunity to add anything else they would like to say which hadn't emerged so far; and finally to put any last questions.It should be made clear to everyone when they can expect to be contacted.

It is generally agreed that the interview is of maximum benefit when other selection methods are also being used. This usually means some form of testing. For a good introduction to testing see reference Toplis *et al.* (1991). Generally speaking there are four types of test you might want to use:

- general intelligence tests
- special aptitude tests (e.g. literacy/numeracy)
- personality tests
- attainment/achievement tests (based around tasks/skills required by the job).

The first three tests would need to be administered by professionally qualified psychologists. But the last kind of test you could devise yourself depending on the kind of competences/competencies you have identified. It is also linked to another selection method called *situational interviews* which is where applicants are asked how they would deal with a particular job-related situation.

If you look back to the second scenario outlined in section 5.1 you will notice that the candidate had to complete a test on numeracy (special aptitude) and a personality test. But they were also required to write a report on how they would propose marketing a particular facility. This was further built on when the applicant had to join a group and the group had to agree on one strategy. This combines a number of testing techniques — aptitude (report writing, interpersonal skills of working in a group), attainment (knowledge of facility, marketing). If it was followed by a question and answer session it would become a situational interview.

A combination of practical job-related tests, psychometric tests, group projects and individual interviews can all be delivered and assessed in what are called *assessment centres*. In a way the word 'centre' is inappropriate because though some large companies *have* set up locations in which such assessment takes place, 'an assessment centre is a process not a place.'[2] Woodruffe (1994) provides a good introduction to creating an assessment centre — the key is not the centre but the *competences* which enable you to design specific tests and simulations to assess.[7]

A survey of MBA students' perception of selection techniques had assessment centres rated top for usefulness and fairness. 'This is not surprising since it typically combines the strengths of other techniques: the apparent "objectivity" of tests and simulations… together with the opportunity for dialogue provided by interviews and debrief sessions'.[8]

Assessment centres are usually associated with the selection of management — mainly because of the cost of setting up a day of the kind illustrated in our second scenario (*see* section 5.1). But as organisations become flatter and distinctions between jobs break down, a company should be looking for a *central and strategic* approach to selection that is appropriate for *all* positions regardless of rank or position in a hierarchy (however flat). We suggest that the principle of openness outlined in section 5.1 is best served by the processes underpinning the design of techniques which collectively go to make up the assessment centre *process*.

To end this section we have compiled a set of selection assessment techniques which might be used to select the person for the role advertised in Figure 4.3 of Chapter 4; these are listed in Figure 5.3

	TECHNIQUES/METHODS			
	Practical Demonstration	Brain storm	Pool-staff meeting	Situational interview
Max score	10	10	10	10
COMPETENCES				
Swimming	*			
Life-saving	*			
Strength	*			
Creativity		*		
Team member			*	
Communication				*
Sensitivity (disabled)				*

Figure 5.3 Assessment centre process for selecting new member of Ajax Pool

Note that to assess the applicant's ability to be a member of the team we have suggested that all members of the pool team (i.e. successful candidates' work colleagues) should be allowed to meet each applicant and assess their suitability as far as working in a team is concerned. Just as a job should be defined in terms of the organisation (*see* Chapter 3), the effectiveness of a person in effecting a role will depend increasingly on their ability to work as a member of a team. This is particularly true of the leisure industry as our six case studies reflect. It is sensible therefore to allow the existing team members to have a say in the selection of a potential colleague.

You will also notice that each method has been allocated a maximum 'score' of ten. This is the other aspect of the assessment centre process — there has to be a standardised marking schedule that potential assessors can agree in judging performance. This need not be complicated. What it does mean is that all members have agreed in advance *how* they are going to assess. In the case of the person specification illustrated in Figure 5.2 a rating scale of 1–6 has been allocated to each characteristic for interviewers to use. The interviewers would have agreed beforehand how to use the scale to rate each characteristic. There is also provision for a weighting to be given to key elements.

With practice you will be able to work out a fair system of allocating marks. As we shall see, more and more assessment is going to become an everyday part of the working day (*see* Chapter 8).

5.4 Examples of good practice

Oasis
We have already seen an example of a common format used by the leisure centre to assess new staff (Figure 5.2). It is based very much on the Rodger's 7-point plan.

Beaulieu
In Chapter 4 we saw how **Beaulieu** uses its open day not only to recruit but also to select staff. Before attending the one-day event applicants will have completed an application form. In effect the one-day event uses an assessment centre approach. During the course of the day potential applicants have to:

- give a one-minute presentation which is tape recorded
- complete a group projec
- complete some simple wordsearch and number tests
- have an interview with the Personnel Manager.

All this is enough to give the Personnel Manager enough evidence of who will best fit into the **Beaulieu** experience. As the Personnel Manager says: 'The people I need most are usually the people who like **Beaulieu** best — it's not just a question of *their* fitting in — *we've* got to fit them as well. I'm looking for people I feel will be happy here.'

5.5 Lessons to be learned

1. The way you organise your selection gives candidates a clue to the kind of organisation they will be joining. By its very nature some may well self-select themselves *out* as the Personnel Managers at the **Oasis** and **MOMI** (*see* Chapter 5) would confirm. In this

respect, providing a realistic opportunity for applicants to experience what it will be like to work with you could be the best form of selection.

2.	All organisations were very clear *what* they wanted from successful applicants and this was equally clearly communicated to them as part of the selection process.

3.	The selection process is the *beginning* of the induction of the employee into the organisation's culture (as in **Beaulieu**'s combination of selection and induction in 4.3 and 4.4). The same is true at **Pleasureland**, where even disappointed application candidates write in to thank the company for the trouble it took over the selection process!

5.6 Action plan

1. Bring together all the information you have about a particular job/role:
    — competence/competency profile (Chapter 3)
    — type of person fitting into the organisations' culture (Chapter 4) and draw up a person specification (as above).

2. If you are sending out an application form check that it asks applicants to provide the key information identified in item 1.

3. On the basis of applications received produce a short-list of six to eight candidates who best meet criteria.

4. For each key competence (occupational standard) and competency (personal characteristic) identify an appropriate way of testing applicants by compiling a matrix as illustrated in Figure 5.3.

5. Ensure that applicants who are seen in person are very clear about the criteria against which they are being assessed and receive feedback whether they are offered the job or not.

6. Ensure that at each stage applicants who do not satisfy respective criteria are informed as soon as possible after the decision has been made.

It has already been suggested that a comprehensive selection process is almost like going on a training programme. For a new member of staff the selection process experience is the first stage of their induction into your company. As we saw **Beaulieu** actually calls its open day an induction day.

But once a person has been accepted to fulfil a given role the onus is on you to ensure they are not only equipped to carry out that role but are also enabled to literally add value to the organisation. This can only be achieved by a programme of continuous learning and development. This is the subject of Chapter 6.

5.7 References

1. Herriot, P. and Fletcher, C. (1990) Candidate-friendly selection for the 1990s *Personnel Management* February 1990, pp. 34 and 32, IPM.

2. Fowler, A. (1992) How to plan an assessment centre *Personnel Management Plus* Vol. 3, no. 12, p. 22, December 1992, IPM.

3. Rodger, A. (1952) *The Seven Point Plan* NIIP.

4. Fowler, A. (1991) How to conduct interviews effectively *Personnel Management Plus* Vol. 2, No. 8, August 1991.

5. Courtis, J. (1988) *Interviews: Skills and Strategies* IPM.

6. Toplis, J., Dulewicz, V. and Fletcher, C. (1991) *Psychological Testing: a manager's guide* IPM.

7. Woodruffe, C. (1994) A*ssessment Centres: Identifying and Developing Competence* 2nd edition IPM.

8. Mabey, C. and Iles, P. (1991) HRM from the other side of the fence *Personnel Management* February 1991.

6. A policy for training and development and continuous learning

6.1 The principles

> *By any measure there is a need for radical reform of our training system. We recognise the commercial necessity of reskilling people and the central importance of linking training plans with business plans.[1]*

This challenge was put forward in a Government White Paper 'Employment for the nineties' which reorganised the shape of training in this country. Out went the old Industry Training Boards established in the 1960s to set national standards for specific industry sectors (e.g. distributive trades, food and drink etc.) and in came Training & Enterprise Councils (TECs) whose remit was to work with businesses in local communities to enure that national initiatives (e.g. Youth Training) met local needs.

Ironically the problems we face in the nineties are not that dissimilar to those faced in the sixties which brought in the Industry Training Boards: for example, skills shortages and inadequate training being carried out by companies. To be fair ITBs have ensured that *more* time and resources are spent by companies on training. But the central question remains — what is the *result* of carrying out such training? Unless, as the quotation above implies, training input can be seen to contribute to business output all the hype about the need to train will be wasted. Consequently TECs are charged with helping companies to see a direct link between training and business success. As we shall see this is the rationale behind the initiative 'Investor in People' (*see* Chapter 10).

I have written elsewhere about the need for an essentially strategic direction for training and development.[2] In this chapter we will explore the implications and applications of just two principles which we believe have very practical consequences.

First we need to be very clear as to what we mean by 'training':

> a <u>planned process</u> to <u>modify</u> attitude, knowledge, or skill behaviour <u>through learning experience</u> to <u>achieve effective performance</u> in an activity or range of activities. Its purpose in the work situation is to develop the abilities of the individual and to satisfy the current and future manpower needs of the organisation.[3]

This came from the Government's Glossary of Training Terms in 1981 but both of our principles are contained within it (in underlined text). The second sentence also anticipates the purpose of training and development which the Training Development Lead Body defines as to 'develop human potential to assist organisations and individuals to achieve their objectives'.

The first principle is that training, by definition, is about *change* which results in a specifiable *outcome*, which could be a demonstrable change in knowledge, attitude or behaviour. As we have seen in Chapter 3 there is now a national movement to define occupational standards in *output* terms for all occupations. As we also saw from Chapter 3 these outputs derive from *purpose* — a job, a task is only a means to an end.

Where training has failed in the past is to focus too much on *input*, i.e. how it should be carried out, and not enough on output. (As we shall see below it *is* the nature of the output that helps to design the input). Not surprisingly a consequence of this strategy (or lack of it!) has been the difficulty in making a connection between training input and individual or organisational objectives.

The second principle relates to the nature of the training itself, the input. If we were to ask you what is the first thing that comes into your mind in response to the word 'training', what would you say? The chances are you would mention 'courses' because that's the way it has often been perceived — attending some kind of formal event. Unfortunately training is still too much associated with the 'attendance' and far less with what resulted from your attendance. With this association also goes this kind of observation about someone who has just returned back to work after attending a training course — 'That's all very well in theory but you can forget all about that now because at work we do it like this...'

The fact is, as the quotation above reminds us, training is essentially a *process* rather than the kind of product described above. The key phrase is 'through *learning* experience'. Have you ever attended a training 'event' which on the face of it was brilliant — well organised, comfortable surroundings, clear overhead transparencies (i.e. you could read them!), an excellent presenter — but as you drove home you weren't sure at all just what, if anything, you had learned? The moral is that if you can't articulate and demonstrate exactly what it is you have learned — you *haven't* been trained.

Slowly, the emphasis is being placed more on *learning* because learning is about the ability to *change* and this ability is being increasingly perceived by industry as the key to survival and success in the future:

> *The ability on which training depends — the ability to specify appropriate behaviour, the necessity of stipulating the conditions under which that behaviour is to be produced, the assumption that what is specified now will hold in ten, five or two years — no longer obtains for most of us. In conditions of rapid change, well trained people (in the limited sense of the word) may become a liability rather than an asset. Now we need people who can flex and adapt quickly, who develop complex and personal repetoires of skills and responses which enable them to get by and survive.*[4]

This may come as a shock to you as you prepare your training programme for the next season, but consider the underlying *principle*. The key to development, change, is the ability to *learn*. In your organisation you need to ensure that everyone is learning all the time — not just when they start with you (though as we shall see in section 6.3 that is a crucial time for development). But in order to have an impact on your organisation individuals' *ability* to learn must be *demonstrated* in some way as affecting change (whether it be individual behaviour, effect on others — e.g. customers — or new ideas which can transform the business). We pick all this up again in Chapter 10.

Professional bodies are also beginning to insist that members practise 'continuing professional development' (CPD). In a few years' time it will no longer be sufficient to take examinations (including practical assessment) at one period in your life and get membership for life. Professional bodies will want to see 'evidence' that you have kept yourself up to date with new developments — which links with the philosophy of competences discussed in Chapter

3. The Institute of Personnel Management (IPM), for example, has made it a condition of upgrading of membership that an individual demonstrates evidence of continuous professional development.[5] Figure 6.1 gives an example of how this evidence could be collected for a member of the staff of Ajax Leisure Pool.

What did you do?	What did you learn?	How might you use this now and in future?
Attended one-day workshop on health and safety	New European Directives (e.g. on lifting)	I've produced a briefing note and suggestions for action which will be discussed at next Health and Safety Committee
Gym instructor demonstrated use of new equipment	How my 10–12 year old group could use it	Will add it to their training schedules and encourage them to show to their parents so they might be tempted to try it for themselves
Read circulated note about potentially hazardous drugs	Not a lot! Went to see Joe who explained it all to me — and side-effects	I'm going to show a video to my 10–12 year olds on dangerous drugs and at same time give examples mentioned in note
Looked through suggestions received over last six months	Frequent reference to need for play area for youngsters	Why not use this as opportunity not just to find space – but expertise in 'play' therapy. I'd be interested myself to get qualification in this area
Attended Catering Committee	How new organic range will be introduced	Ask for more information and samples so can introduce to my class
Attended meeting of Parent Teachers Association at my son's school	Concern of teachers of lack of fitness of children	I've put a note in the suggestion book about feasibility of running local fitness campaign for schools building on 'Fit Kids' initiative

Figure 6.1 An example of continuous development

Notice also that Figure 6.1 includes evidence of learning that has been derived from *non-vocational* activities. This is another trend — life-long learning. Companies are realising that helping individuals to develop skills *outside* of work can also have a spin-off *inside* work. This is the advantage of taking a wider view of an individual's all round *development* rather than limiting your view to 'training' which by definition is limited to specific objectives. What is transferrable may not be the content of outside development (e.g. pottery, car maintenance, karate) but the *learning* that the individual has realised as a result of engaging in these activities. This learning could relate to self-knowledge, confidence that will further enhance your assets. It is a source of learning that many companies ignore, as a survey into what factors affect companies' training decisions found.[6]

Having followed through the HRM policies outlined in the previous five chapters you should be in a position where you have recruited and selected a member of staff who: can be quickly fitted into an existing job role; is acceptable and can contribute to team work; and who also has potential for growth in the future. Enriched with all this talent you cannot but design a development programme that meets the two principles we have outlined above:

1. That is capable of leading to demonstrable behaviour/output that will contribute to individual, team and organisational objectives.

2. That allows the individual to learn in the most appropriate way to achieve these objectives — i.e. appropriate to individual needs, organisational resources and future requirements.

Before we look at the benefits of such an approach and how you can bring it about, it is interesting to report an observation made by the Director of **Pleasureland** at Southport, which was awarded 'Investor in People' in September 1993. Discussing the kind of manager he wanted to recruit for the future he was adamant that he would not recruit managers from a well-known national fast food company *because* of the training they had received. The training was excellent but it was so tied to the company's particular standards and manuals that without them the manager would be unlikely to adapt to the kind of open, empowered culture that, as we shall see, **Pleasureland** is trying to grow. Sometimes past training can conflict with future needs. We hope your training and development can lead to the realisation of learning that will not only be good for you and the individuals concerned but, in due course will add to the skills of the leisure industry.

6.2 What's in it for me?

1. If you're serious about Human Resource Management, investment in your people will be equally as important as investing in and upgrading other assets — equipment, facilities, etc. Otherwise they will depreciate to the point that you might as well write them off! In the same way as you regularly appraise the value of your other assets you should carry out a similar audit of your staff. As we saw in Chapter 3 the introduction of a competence-based development scheme into your organisation can literally add value in the workplace which is capable of being assessed.

2. Having spent as much as you have in selecting the right person you want to keep them at least as long as they are able to make a contribution which is worth as much as cost of recruitment. This means from day one they will need a period of induction and development without which you will find they may leave you before they have even begun to make any contribution whatsoever.

3. Quality control: though we may have implied that standards manuals can limit the transferability of skills, they nevertheless can ensure that consistent standards are maintained. As is well known this is even more critical in any customer service. It can also be part of an employee's contract of employment that they will be trained and enabled to meet defined standards. Inability to perform satisfactorily could lead to dismissal.

4. Legal obligation. The obverse of item 3 is that if you *have* dismissed an employee for not performing satisfactorily and they can prove that they never received training they can claim unfair dismissal. Also, in an industry where safety is paramount you have major obligations under the Health and Safety at Work Act

to train staff to meet safety standards. Staff in your catering outlets will also need training to meet requirements of food and hygiene legislation. These areas are covered more fully in Chapter 2.

5. A training policy that clearly links training and development of *every* employee with the goals of your business is the basis for the 'Investor in People' award (Chapter 10).

6. If your organisation is to have a future it will depend on two things: an external market that needs your services and is prepared and able to purchase it; and employees that are able to provide the service customers expect and are able to adapt their skills to meet changing demands, needs — whatever their source. The creation of such a creative, flexible workforce cannot but be achieved by defining, encouraging and facilitating *learning* at every level and celebrating the outcome. This is the basis for the Learning Organisation which we discuss in the Conclusions to this book. The starting point is to evolve a policy on learning and development which is accessible to all.

6.3 What's involved?

A legacy of the Industry Training Boards was to provide industry with a standard framework within which training needs could be identified, met and recorded. The framework was called systematic training and involved a four-stage cycle which could be applied to anyone in any job, this is reproduced in Figure 6.2.

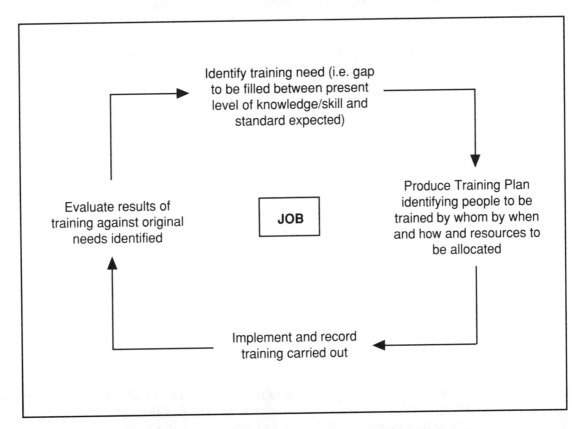

Figure 6.2 The four-stage cycle of systemic training

When you come to explore the Investor in People scheme in Chapter 10, you will see that there is some similarity between its criteria and the above stages of systematic training. The main difference is that Investor in People is all about demonstrating a link between training input and business outcomes. Though the 'evaluation' stage of the systematic training cycle in theory provided an opportunity to make a similar connection, all too often ITBs were mainly interested in inspecting that training had been carried out rather than questioning the outcome. Nevertheless they did lay a foundation for the *recording* of training.

As we shall see from examples of records kept by our case study organisations, there is a similarity between them which reflects the need to record basic data for all members of staff. In Chapter 7 the process for identifying training and development needs is shown, usually, to be some form of one-to-one appraisal between boss and subordinate. But our starting point is the stage we reached at the end of Chapter 5 — a new member of staff has been recruited and selected. How are they enabled to become a productive member of staff as quickly as possible? This is the immediate problem that your Training Policy should address.

The Director of **Pleasureland** recalls with amazement the situation he was faced with when he took over the amusement park from the local council. Staff were recruited and almost immediately put to work on rides with little or no introduction to the job. He contrasts this with the system now in place of one-day company induction, followed by departmental induction and specific job training. Training can be divided up into the following types:

Induction: Arrangements are made by or on behalf of the management to familiarise the new employee with the working organisation, welfare and safety matters, general conditions of employment and the work of the department in which he is employed.[7]

Specific job training A new member of staff is introduced to a specific job and enabled to reach the necessary standard of performance. This maybe through on-job coaching by an experienced member of staff trained as a trainer and/or through an external trainer or arranged training event/s.

Continuous training/ development This can take a number of forms:

1. Regular review of employee's performance and identification of further training needs. These could be of three kinds:
   - Need for *remedial* training to improve performance/knowledge.
   - Need for *up-dating* in new procedure/skill required for the future.
   - Need for *development* whereby employee is prepared for new job; this might involve attendance of external courses and/or provision of on-job opportunities for them to take on new responsibilities.

2. Identification of needs affecting all members of staff requiring everyone to receive the same training.

Examples of all these types of training are given when we examine good practice from our case studies. But first we want you to go back to the two underlying principles we identified. Training is about change which has to be precisely defined if it is to be realised and if an individual (and organisation) is able to learn from it. A central issue for us is who *owns* the results of the training.

For sometime there has been a debate in the training world as to the difference between 'training' and 'development'. It has been suggested that training is something 'done for you or to you' whereas development is self-directed.[4] I take the view that for *learning*, real learning to occur by definition, the individual *must* take ownership for their own development.

The resources they draw upon, as we shall see, are rich and varied and will *include* all the types of training provision listed above. But at the end of the day only the employee can confirm that they *have* been trained, developed by providing *evidence* of the learning they have realised.

The records that ITBs inspected were very often simply a record of training *being provided* (i.e. input) and not of *learning realised* (output). Some of the records illustrated over the following pages are of this kind but some also see the need to recognise the *achievement* outcome. To a large extent the focus on competences, discussed in Chapter 3, and demonstrations of achievement in the workplace will create a new kind of learning culture whereby everyone takes ownership for their *own* development and is consciously seeking to get their own learning recognised; a point which is developed in the overall conclusion to the book. The fact that many universities are now also recognising and accrediting what is called 'work-based learning' means that employees will be able to gain academic qualifications at all levels by demonstrating, through presentation of a portfolio, evidence specific learning derived from work-based experience. (I am a member of Middlesex University's National Centre for Work-Based Learning Partnerships and would be happy to advise readers on how to go about getting accreditation for work-based-learning.)

But this kind of learning will not happen automatically. As a manager you have the opportunity of developing a training and development policy to help all your employees translate training input into learning output. The form in Figure 6.1 is an example of how this can be achieved. If every new employee is presented with a development log in this format as soon as they join they can be encouraged to write up *for themselves* how they have learned from experiences at work, attendance of courses and even outside events.

In the Action Plan you will be asked to follow through a number of steps to create a development policy at the heart of which is an individual development log. Recorded in that log are outputs (evidence). You will also be asked to review the training you already provide in relation to how it helps the learner translate what is covered in the training into a personal action plan which will be the basis for continuing development.

So far we have concentrated on one of the two principles we started with, that any training and development you provide is capable of leading to demonstrable behaviour/output that will contribute to individual, team and organisational objectives. The implications of the second principle are just as important: that the form the training/development takes allows the individual to learn in the most appropriate way to achieve these objectives — i.e. appropriate to individual needs, organisational resources and future requirements.

In designing any training or development event I suggest there are four components which I have described elsewhere as 'the learning mix'.[2] Below we look at these four components in relation to the development plan illustrated in Figure 6.1.

Individual learning style   We each learn in a different way. There is a learning inventory you can obtain which will help you identify your preferred way of learning.[8] From the example in Figure 6.1 it seems this person enjoys learning in groups from practical problems. They don't appear to learn much from reading.

Interventionist role of tutor/trainer/mentor   Some people *are* natural trainers or tutors — but most of us can be helped to train, develop others. In Figure 6.3 is a summary of the key skills involved in one-to-one coaching

---

1.   Getting learners's attention
1.1   *Explain* clearly what has to be done.
1.2   *Give reason* for completing task.
1.3   Make task *interesting*.

2.   Introducing task
2.1   *Demonstrate* complete task.
2.2   *Explain* what has to be done and why.

3.   Break down of task
3.1   Break down task *step by step* to suit task and learner's ability.
3.2   *Check understanding* at each stage and give feedback as necessary.
3.3   *Give positive feedback and encouragement* at each stage.

4.   Consolidation
4.1   *Summarise* at end and *check understanding*.

5.   Check
5.1   Get each trainee to *complete whole task* at end.
5.2   *Give feedback* on how well learner has performed.
5.3   Point out *faults* and give *coaching* as appropriate.

Figure 6.3 Checklist for good instructional practice

There are now national standards for trainers.[9] **Butlins Southcoast World** has a policy that all its supervisors will acquire two of these standards which relate to assessment of evidence for purposes of NVQ accreditation (*see* Chapter 3).

There is an increasing emphasis being placed on the need for every member of staff to have a 'mentor'; this is someone usually other than the person's immediate boss who makes themselves available to support and develop another member of staff.

In the example in Figure 6.1 the person is clearly taking advantage of an experienced member of staff to extend their range of skills. It would be up to the company to identify the role being played by this other person (at appraisal — *see* Chapter 7) and ensure that they are equipped to be mentors and maybe potential NVQ assessors.

Learning resources/media

Most courses use a range of media and methods — Video, case-studies, overhead transparencies, role-play — to help illustrate concepts and give delegates an opportunity to develop skills. Many such media and methods are available for your use *outside* of the classroom situation (e.g. videos, case studies) There are also 'open learning packages' that enable staff to learn and practise new skills by themselves such as 'Focus' training developed by **Bolton Health Studio,** in Section 6.4.

But in addition most organisations have a wealth of material — resources they can draw on that can be used in support of learning.

Most of our case studies have produced employee handbooks which refer to reports, handbooks, manuals which staff can access.

In the example in Figure 6.1 the individual concerned has used the suggestion book as a means of learning how to offer better service.

Organisational context　In the final analysis the *context* in which employees work provides a rich source for learning. This is particularly true of the leisure industry where there is no substitute for live involvement. This is why induction, as we have seen is so critical — because it is able to give new recruits a feel for the culture and environment in which they will be working. **Pleasureland** uses 'emergency' training to dramatic effect in this context, (see Section 6.4).

Briefing meetings, which most of our case studies use to cascade a message down the line, can be turned into an opportunity for learning. The example in Figure 6.1 shows how a meeting was a source of learning. For details of a range of 'learning opportunities' at work *see* Honey and Mumford (1989).

It is not possible in this chapter to review the wide range of techniques and methods you can use to train and develop your staff. Both Reid, Barrington and Kenny (1992) and Anderson (1993) can be used for guidance in training in general and Mumford (1993) for management development). Our objective is to enable you to see training and development as an *ongoing* commitment to enable your staff to realise the potential you saw in them when you recruited them. Before you begin to design your training strategy you should remember the two principles that should underpin everything: the training/development should be such that:

- it is capable of leading to demonstrable behaviour/output that will contribute to individual, team and organisational objectives
- it allows the individual to learn in the most appropriate way to achieve these objectives — i.e. appropriate to individual needs, organisational resources and future requirements.

To achieve this you should commit specific resources of time and money. If you wish to be considered for an 'Investor in People' award (*see* Chapter 10), you will need to identify the specific resources allocated to meeting training and development needs and the responsibilities of designated members of staff (especially managers) for developing their staff. In Figure 6.3 you can see the training and development policy of **Pleasureland**.

Within your organisation you have a range of resources available to you for the development of staff. We have divided them into four.

First, don't forget that each individual is a resource unto themselves and has their own preferred learning style if they are encouraged to recognise and use it.

Second, everyone *could* be developed to develop others but initially it is appropriate to train a designated group of staff (probably supervisors/managers) in basic techniques (*see* Figure 6.3).

Third, your organisation will have a rich source of materials that can be presented/organised in such a way as to encourage learning: reports, magazines, videos, handouts, manuals, etc.

1. **The company commitment**

   The Company and Directors of the company are fully committed to investing in our people for the benefit of the business and allowing individuals to reach their full potential.

   We are an equal opportunities employer. Decisions about training and development will be made irrespective of race, gender, religion, disability or age.

2. **Responsibilities**

   Both you and your Line Manager share the responsibility for identifying your training needs. The Group Training Manager and your Park Senior management are responsible for implementing this policy.

   Induction

   All new staff will receive induction training, either as part of a group or by one to one sessions with a Line Manager. All staff will be given a copy of this policy as part of their induction package.

   Health and Safety training

   All staff will undergo health and safety training. Specific training will be given where it is relevant to the job

3. **The overall process**

   How training will be delivered

   Most of your training will be carried out by your immediate Supervisor, usually in the workplace. When necessary, we will provide off-job training delivered by a specialist.

   Identification of training needs

   All new permanent staff will agree a personal development plan with their Line Manager. Performance reviews will be carried out at least once during the season for seasonal staff and at least once annually for permanent staff. A record will be kept of all performance reviews.

   Evaluation of training

   After training has taken place, you will discuss the effectiveness with your Line Manager. For seasonal staff this will be covered during your review and for Permanent staff you will be asked to complete a 'debrief' form.

   Training plans

   Each year the Group Training Manager will compile a Company Training Plan from individual development plans of permanent staff and from consultation with Line Management for the seasonal staff. The plan will be signed off at each level in the organisation and approved by the Board of Directors

   Nationally recognised qualifications

   Where appropriate training will lead to nationally recognised qualifications.

   Signed..

   Group Training Manager

Figure 6.4 Example of Training Policy distributed to all staff at Pleasureland

Finally and most importantly it is the kind of *culture* your organisation has that will encourage learning. This could be using day-to-day meetings as a basis for encouraging individual action and development, as in Figure 6.1. It could be to 'open' up your facilities in such a way that people can continually update themselves on what you are about. Traditionally this happens during induction. As we report below the 'open day' is particularly well used in the leisure industry — perhaps it could also be available to *existing* staff as well as new ones.

But now it is time to explore the range of approaches used by our case studies to develop staff and record the results.

6.4 Examples of good practice

Rather than take each case study in turn we will work through examples that relate to the various stages in designing appropriate training and development we have so far highlighted starting with training policy.

Company training policy

We have already drawn attention to the policy of **Pleasureland,** Figure 6.4, as an example of the kind of company commitment to developing all staff and resources to be made available. Most of the case studies had their own form of communicating to staff just how they would be developed.

Company training plan

Those companies that have received the 'Investors in People' award (**Butlins Southcoast World**, **Torquay Leisure Hotels** and **Pleasureland**) have all produced a summary of the training needs to be met in a given year based on individual appraisals (*see* Chapter 7). For example, in Figure 6.5 is the format **Pleasureland** used to summarise training needs of permanent members of staff following their appraisal in 1992.

Training needs 1993

As a result of the November/December 1992 Appraisals for all permanent employees at Pleasureland, Southport, the following training needs were highlighted. Where no formal training is listed as being necessary, please note that ALL employees have been set objectives for the forthcoming year which are considered to be attainable without formal training

Employee and training needs	To be actioned by	Comments and date to be actioned

---

Figure 6.5 Pleasureland's summary of training needs

Some of the needs were common to a number of individuals, e.g. health and safety awareness, first aid, and were covered by a single formal event; others were individually specific (e.g. assertiveness training) and were best suited to individual development (in this case a video and debrief session).

Induction

We have already had cause to give an example of the one-day event at **Beaulieu** in Chapter 4 on Recruitment. In the leisure industry, an open day to recruit seasonal staff often doubles up as an induction day. The same is true at **Pleasureland**. In Figure 6.6 is a summary of the day and the questions that are posed to staff as part of a Treasure Hunt.

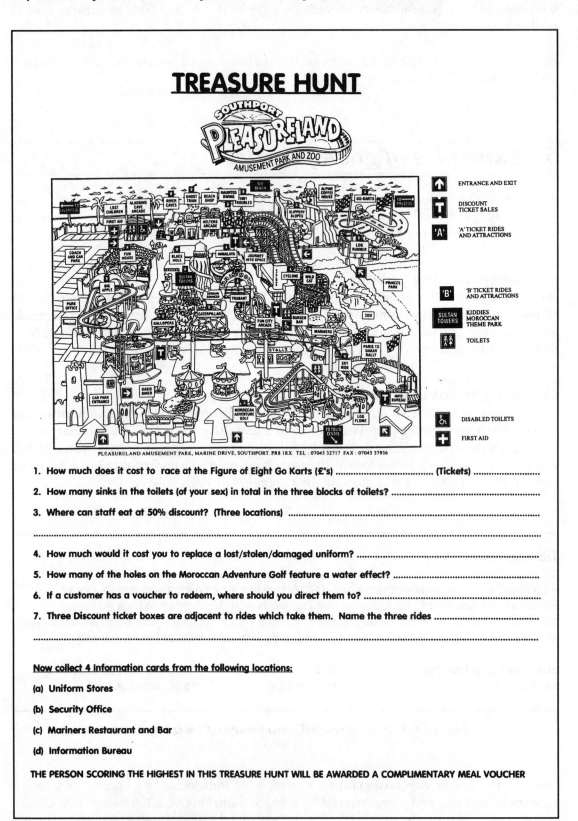

Figure 6.6 Staff treasure hunt at Pleasureland

Gone are the days when induction simply meant new staff sitting down and listening to long speeches on organisational policy. Induction in the leisure industry, as our case studies show, is fun and involves as many activities as possible. The emphasis is on the *employee* finding out and learning for themselves. But this also means that existing staff and managers are adequately briefed beforehand to support 'inductees' to gather information they need. **Pleasureland** provides involved members of staff with a briefing pack for this purpose. It also provides a 'welcome pack' which for permanent staff includes:

- Organisation chart.
- Letter of welcome from the MD, and Training Manager.
- Contract of employment.
- Job description.
- Health and safety fact sheet.
- Facts sheets relevant to job.
- Employees' handbook.
- First day at work checklist.
- History of Pleasureland.
- Details of appraisal scheme.

In addition to an induction to **Pleasureland** as a company new members of staff also receive an induction to the particular department in which they will be working. This leads on to specific job training

Specific job training

One of the criteria of Investor in People (IiP) (*see* Chapter 10) is that 'all new employees are introduced effectively to the organisation and are given the training and development needed to do their jobs'. Assessors of IiP would want to see evidence that each member of staff has received the necessary training to do the job. In effect this is done by training check-lists which identify specific activities and require the employee's supervisor to verify that the training has been carried out satisfactorily. Figure 6.7 presents an example of an individual training record from **Pleasureland** for employees in the Arcades and Games department.

Notice that the company asks for the parent company's Group Training Officer (GTO) to carry out an audit that records are being kept up to date. This is an interesting 'internalisation' of the functions once undertaken by the Industry Training Boards.

Butlins Southcoast World has a very well defined 'Five Star' development programme for each employee. One star is awarded after completing induction, two stars for completion of basic job skills and being judged satisfactorily on their graded appraisal scheme (*see* Chapter 7) and five stars for getting awarded an NVQ. See Figure 6.8 for a description of the Five Star scheme.

However, it is not always possible to break down a work role into such clearly defined performance elements. At **MOMI**, for example, successful performance by each of its 'interpreter' Guides requires, by definition, individual creativity. Each has literally to create two roles based loosely around background information about a particular character and period of history (e.g. Commissionaire of Odeon in the forties). To become proficient the actor is given background reading and required to attend a series of seminars but is also expected to do personal research and evolve a character of their own in the company of fellow 'interpreters' and working individually with the Director to perfect the role. The training is very thorough — three weeks — and resulted in **MOMI** being awarded a National Training Award in 1992.

SOUTHPORT PLEASURELAND
THE AMUSEMENT PARK ON THE SANDS

DEPARTMENT: <u>ARCADES AND GAMES</u>   Name: ----------------------------------

Job title: --   Start date: -------------------------------

Finish date: -------------------------------

UNITS	Date	Signature of trainee	Signature of trainer	Training assessed by	Comments by assessor
Park induction					
Health & safety					
Departmental induction					
Opening procedure					
Closing procedure					
Empty procedure (games)					
Empty procedure (arcades)					
Refloat procedure (arcades)					
Metering procedure (arcades)					
Float procedure (arcades)					
Fire training					
Forgery training					
Stock training					
Customer care					
Cleaning					
Presentation					

Audited by G.T.O.: ----------------------------- (signature) ------------------------------- (date)

Figure 6.7 Pleasureland training record

OPERATIVE LEVEL STARS

Job Grade A

One Star Level plus Certificate of Course Completion
— After completion of STARS Introduction and Department STARS, which shall include the Company Internal Food Hygiene Course.

Two Star Level plus Certificate of Competence
— One star gained.
— Completion of Basic Job Skills training (must be blue books modules when available) and satisfactorily assessed by immediate boss and verified by an assessor qualified in TDLB units D32 and D33.
— Satisfactory appraisal with immediate boss — Section A on the Appraisal Form must have the following scores:
  – Overall Performance Assessment — minimum grade of B3 in all categories, no Cs.
(Usually at the end of 4 weeks from date of commencement).

Three Star level
— Two stars gained.
— Satisfactory appraisal with immediate boss.
— Section A in the Appraisal Form must have the following scores:
  – Overall Performance assessment — minimum of 4 B2s no Cs.
  – Performance Against Targets — minimum of 2 B2s, no Cs.
(Usually at the end of 8 weeks from date of commencement).

Four Star Level
— Three stars gained.
— Satisfactory appraisal with immediate boss.
— Section A in the Appraisal Form must have the following scores:
  – Overall Performance Assessment — minimum of 4 B1s, no B3s, no Cs.
  – Performance Against Targets — minimum of 2 B1s, no B3s, no Cs.
(Usually at the end of 12 weeks from date of commencement).

Five Star Level plus Certificate of Excellence
— Four Stars gained.
— Completion of NVQ level 2 where appropriate (NVQs offered at Butlins are Retail certificate, Hospitality and Catering, Business Administration as standard and are available in Administration, Shops, Retail Catering, Bars, Accommodation, Customer catering, Reception).
— Satisfactory Appraisal by immediate boss.
— Section A in the Appraisal Form must have the following scores:
  – Overall Performance Assessment — minimum of 4 As, no B2s. no B3s, no Cs.
  – Performance Against Targets — minimum of 2As, no B2s, no B3s, no Cs.
(Usually after 16 weeks from date of commencement).

Figure 6.8 Butlins Southcoast World's Five Star recognition scheme (extract)

In 1991 **Bolton Health Studio** received a National Training Award for its **Focus Training**. For 25 years the studio had been involved in training fitness instructors. In the absence of national standards for fitness instruction it saw the opportunity of creating a learning package that could be worked through individually and would prepare an individual to be assessed at a centre of their choice. The resulting package, Focus Training, comprises a work manual (summarising in attractive format the necessary theory), a video (illustrating the practice) and an audio-cassette (which gives personal accounts of what it is like to be an instructor). All staff at the **Bolton Health Studio** are put through the package and required to meet a satisfactory standard of assessment.

Continuous job training/development

Following on from initial job training, the emphasis, as we have seen, is very much now on continuous development. It is also a criterion to be met in 'Investor in People' schemes: 'The skills of existing employees are developed in line with business objectives.' Furthermore another criterion requires that 'all employees are made aware of the development opportunities open to them'.

Most of our case studies had an ongoing provision of training sessions, some in-house, some external, the content and dates of which were circulated to all employees. The most common subjects for regular attention are health and safety, security and customer relations.

Bolton Health Studio requires supervisors to spend one hour of every day training a member of their staff. It has also run *ad hoc* events for everyone. The latest event has been two sessions on neuro-linguistic programming one of which had to be attended by *every* member of staff.

Pleasureland creates an 'emergency' scenario in which all staff are expected to be involved. The latest situation involved two terrorist bombs being planted in different locations in the amusement park and involved co-operation of the fire, ambulance and police services which were happy to co-operate as it also afforded them a training opportunity that would be difficult to simulate. The event was followed by a debriefing session to take account of lessons learned.

6.5 Lessons to be learned

1. All case studies without exception have given training and development a very high priority. They have paid particular attention to the importance of *induction* to be followed by *specific job training* which is recorded and used in appraisal of performance (*see* Chapter 7). There is also evidence for the need of *continuous* training particularly in the fields of health and safety, security and customer relations

2. Evidence of innovative use of training methods to fit particular circumstances is provided by two of the case studies which have won National Training Awards for their application. We would also draw your attention to the 'emergency' practice recently introduced at **Pleasureland**.

3. On the whole the emphasis is on the recording of training provided rather than on lessons learned. There are two examples of the latter: **Butlins Southcoast World** encourages staff to use their job training to build up a portfolio of evidence that can be used to acquire an NVQ — *see* Chapter 3 . **Bolton Health Studio's** Focus Training enables staff to take ownership of their own development as instructors and seek assessment when they are ready. It is but a small step from providing training to helping individuals take ownership for their own development. The kind of format illustrated in Figure 6.1 can enable everyone to make this transition and can also be extended so that it leads to NVQs as shown in Chapter 3. The Action Plan that follows also suggests a strategy for making this transition.

6.6 Action plan

1. Look back to your response to the Action Plan after Chapter 3, where you reviewed the range of functions that need to be carried out in your organisation and how these could be broken down into competences. As a result you should have identified some core competences which are common to a number of roles, functions and other competences specific to particular roles. These competences are the outcomes that new and current staff must be able to demonstrate. Your Training and Development Plan should indicate *how* you will enable your staff to meet these competences (which in turn should be related to your business goals). In your Action Plan you will find a framework within which to record the outcome from the following activities.

2. Against the list of competences identify how you currently train staff to achieve them (e.g. training courses, one-to-one coaching by supervisor, etc.). Now identify additional/ alternative methods you might use (refer back to range the of methods introduced in section 6.3).

3. As an alternative check on effective use of training, review every course, training event you offer by identifying objectives of course/event and what *evidence* there is of individuals being able to apply what has been learned. For example, you might offer a course on 'carrying out appraisal', as a result of which a supervisor learns a systematic approach to carrying out appraisal but you need to know if this is followed up and evidence provided as to its application: e.g. evidence that the supervisor has since carried out appraisal satisfactorily as confirmed by the appraisee.

4. Having carried out a company-wide review of core competences that need to be covered, and reviewed effectiveness of training resources in meeting them, all you have to identify now is *who* needs developing in what. New starters will need induction and *may* need individual training depending on competences already held. (Once everyone becomes accustomed to keeping a portfolio this will make it easier for new employers to find out existing levels of competence and therefore further development needed.) Existing staff may or may not need individual training depending on the outcome of a performance review (*see* Chapter 7).

5. You should now be able to complete details under headings Induction and Specific Job Training.

6. Now consider 'on-going' development needs. Refer back to the earlier chapters when you identified your mission (Chapter 1), and external factors that could affect your employees. For example, new legislation, need to focus on new market ('fit kids'?). Complete accordingly.

7. What you've produced so far should give you an overview of the basic training and development you need to provide to ensure you meet your goals. You should be able to estimate the kind of costs involved to provide these resources. This should include the costs of a record and administrative system to monitor its effectiveness, to which we now turn.

8. The key records are as follows:

    — **Training policy.** (Which we are going to leave to the end once we have identified the range of factors you need to take into account.)

    — **Training Plan.** This is what you've completed. It summarises the overall company commitment of resources 'on what' and 'for whom' 'by when' and 'how'.

— **Individual Training Records**. Each employee should have an individual record of the kind illustrated in Figures 6.4 and 6.6 which records in chronological order all training and development received from day one of joining the company. If you do not already have such records we would recommend you link them with individual portfolios of achievement.

— **Individual portfolios and records of achievement.** Right from the outset of this chapter we have encouraged you to help individual staff take ownership for their *own* development. You will, of course, need to keep records of what development you have provided but you should also enable every member of staff maintain from day one their own development log (of kind illustrated in Figure 6.1). This has two key advantages:

1. It helps the individual recognise their own value. It comes in two parts, the form illustrated in Figure 6.1 is really a summary of what the individual has learned. The portfolio would contain the actual evidence (e.g. in relation to Figure 6.1, actual notes on health and safety, hazardous drugs, proposals for fitness campaign). It is the portfolio of evidence that can be used in support of NVQs (*see* Chapter 3).

2. It can be used to 'add value' to the organisation. This is the key to the learning organisation that we look at in the conclusions section. The individual portfolio is your record of the *real* learning that is being realised in your organisation. If only you could tap that you really *would* be a learning organisation.

9. Finally, reflecting on what you plan to do above, you can put together the rationale for your approach in a training policy (Figure 6.4 is an example). Above all it should reflect the commitment of your company to development in terms of resources to be allocated (money and people). In particular it should identify which staff will be responsible for developing others and what development support they will get.

Before finalising your training policy you might like to read Chapter 7 whose theme of appraisal and evaluation is inextricably linked with one of the principles we started out with — training/learning *must* lead to a measurable outcome. Part of your Policy should indicate just how you will ensure that outcome is evaluated.

6.7 References

1. Department of Employment (1988) *Employment for the 1990s* HMSO.

2. Critten, P. (1993) *Investing in People: Towards Corporate Capability* Butterworth-Heinemann.

3. Manpower Services Commission (1981) *Glossary of training Terms* HMSO.

4. Boydell, T., Leary, N. and Pedler, P. (1993) Crossing the threshold: the challenge facing trainers, developers and line managers *Transition* January 1993, p. 12.

5. IPM News (1993) A satisfactory record of learning *Personnel Managememnt Plus* Vol. 4, No. 9, September 1993, p. 36.

6. Rainbird, H. and Maguire, M. (1993) When corporate need supersede employee development *Personnel Management* February 1993.

7. Department of Employment (1971) *Glossary of Training Terms* HMSO.

8. Honey, P. and Mumford, A. (1992) *The Manual of Learning Styles* Honey.

9. Training and Development Lead Body (1992) *National Standards for Training and Development* Department of Employment.

10. Clutterbuck, D. (1991) *Everyone Needs a Mentor — Fostering Talent at Work* IPM.

11. Honey, P. and Mumford, A. (1989) *The Manual of Learning opportunities* Honey.

12. Anderson, A. (1993) *Successful Training Practice — A Manager's Guide to Personnel Development* Blackwell.

13. Reid, N., Barrington, H. and Kenney, J. (1992) *Training Interventions* 3rd edition IPM.

14. Mumford, A. (1993) *Management Development: Strategies for Action* 2nd edition, IPM

15. Fairbairns, J. (1991) Plugging the gap in training needs analysis *Personnel Management* February 1991, pp. 43–45).

7. *Evaluating and appraising performance*

7.1 The principles

An underlying theme throughout this book is that employee and employer can only put a true value on the contribution of people to the organisation's objectives if both are clear about what *output* is expected of them. I believe that the move towards National Occupational Standards and their assessment against National Vocational Qualifications (NVQs) can help employers and managers, despite the criticism of inherent bureaucracy (*see* Chapter 3), establish a *base level* for what can be achieved. This does not and should not mean that the organisation stops there.

This brings us to a second underlying theme of the book: even if you apply each principle, unless you *integrate* them all into an overall strategy and embed them within your company *culture* you will not realise and release their full benefits. The theme of this chapter is just *how* you can put a value on what is achieved and what is achievable in the workplace. This is part of what is being called 'performance management':

> *Performance management can be defined as a process or set of processes for establishing shared understanding about what is to be achieved, and of managing and developing people in a way which increases the probability that it* will *be achieved in the short and longer term.*
>
> *The overall aim of performance management is to establish a culture in which individuals and groups take responsibility for the continuous improvement of business processes, and of their own skills and contributions.*[1]

The process is inextricably linked up with performance related pay (PRP) which we will look at in Chapter 8. But you cannot begin to operate such a system unless you and most importantly your *staff* are very clear about what constitutes satisfactory performance.

The process is also linked up with procedures for carrying out 'appraisal', together with all the attitudes and values that inevitably go with it. As we shall see, one of the concerns often expressed about appraisal is that those undergoing it are often not clear about the performance criteria against which they are being judged and/or how well their appraiser *knows* their performance to be able to make a valid assessment. (For a key source on performance management see reference [14.])

The principles to focus on are:

1. The need for clear standards of performance for every member of staff.

2. A culture which encourages clear *communication* and *sharing* of such standards and *feed-back* to individuals concerned following any appraisal or evaluation.

These principles we suggest equally apply to the evaluation of *training* which, from personal experience of training over 25 years, I know has always been isolated as a problematic area.

An article in *Transition* sums it up under its title: 'The financial return from training and development: hard facts or act of faith?'[2] The direct link between the cost of a particular input of training and a tangible 'bottom-line' financial measure like a '10% increase in customer spend' is the holy grail still devotedly sought by managers who want it to be *proved* to them that investment in training/development is worth their while. The Industry Training Boards, as I know from the years I spent with the Hotel and Catering Training ITB, were never able to *prove* such a connection. They settled for encouraging companies to 'evaluate' their training using some form of questionnaire that gave them feedback about the appropriateness of the training methods used rather than whether the input led to a *valuable output*. They opted for what is known as *formative* evaluation rather than a *summative* approach.

Recognition as an Investor in People, on the other hand, recognises that the very rationale on which it is based requires companies to make a link between training and development input and consequences for business objectives. But it is realistic enough not to expect a cause and effect relationship. The onus is on the company to demonstrate *how* it collects evidence to show the effectiveness of its development programme and how *this* contributes to business objectives (*see* Chapter 10).

 The problem is that historically evaluation of *training* has become the central focus rather than the evaluation of *change* that should result *from* the training. Our view is that this is because organisations have never been clear just what to expect from training and therefore have focused on the input rather than the output.

Writing in an influential book on the evaluation of training (now sadly out of print) 20 years ago Tony Hamblin had this to say:

> *I would predict that before the end of the century it will be impossible to write a book purely about the evaluation of training. Training, except for certain routine tasks, will cease to be a separate organisational activity ... and evaluation (if the word is still being used) will be concerned with the total evaluation of organisational or personal activities rather than training as such...*[3]

Six years to go before the end of the century books on evaluation *are* still appearing but if initiatives like Investor in People is successful the hope is that Tony Hamblin's prediction might prove vindicated. The Action Plan you will be preparing will hopefully also move the emphasis of appraisal and evaluation towards outcomes and a company-wide assessment of the implications for the organisation as a whole.

7.2 What's in it for me?

1. As with any other asset in which you have invested, you will want to see some kind of return. But, unlike other assets, the kind of return you expect needs to be *negotiated* and mutually agreed.

2. Unlike other assets, people can actually *grow in value* through the very process of appraisal and evaluation. Contrary to popular opinion, people *do* like to know what is expected of them, they *do* like to be given feedback about their performance. For one thing it gives them *recognition*; and recognition, as Herzberg discovered,[4] is a key motivator.

3. It can be the basis for performance related pay (*see* Chapter 8). If you create a culture where everyone knows just what everyone else is responsible and accountable for you have a basis for a just system of remuneration.

4. If your performance criteria are linked with national standards (*see* Chapter 3) staff can get NVQ accreditation which gives them added value in the market place.

5. Finally, if everyone has clear targets it makes it easier to manage.

7.3 *What's involved?*

Step 1

The starting point has to be principle one, that there should be performance standards for every member of staff. For some time now, since Peter Drucker published his book *The Practice of Management* in 1954,[5] the concept of 'Management by Objectives' (MBO) has been applied by companies in some form or other. Drucker was the first to draw a distinction between management *efficiency*, which he called 'doing things right' and management *effectiveness* which he called 'doing the right things'.

Management by Objectives was a way of focusing on effectiveness by concentrating on what managers had *achieved* rather than what they did. Management by Objectives is simply the process by which a boss agrees with their subordinate on what needs to be achieved over a given period after which time a date is arranged for boss and subordinate to review success and agree on next set of objectives. What could be simpler?

The problem — as with so many other initiatives — is that unless the scheme is embedded in a culture where there is trust, where unrealistic targets are not imposed on the subordinate from above, it will fail; many companies would recognise these as reasons why the scheme *has* failed. An in-depth review by IPM of performance management in 26 organisations revealed that its success depended on the commitment and ownership of line management.[15]. Too often the scheme was started in response to external pressures rather than as part of an integrated and strategic employee–development approach. But it is a powerful process if two principles are recognised:

1. Targets set must be SMART, that is:
   S — Specific
   M — Measurable
   A — Achievable
   R — Relevant
   T — Timed

2. The targets should ideally be set by the individuals concerned and then agreed with their manager. This embraces two other principles that are in vogue at the moment, 'empowerment' and the Japanese concept of *'kaizen'*. Empowerment is simply the process of allowing individuals to decide for themselves how to tackle specific tasks. All that are set are the outcomes (Compare this approach with the compilation of detailed job descriptions — *see* Chapter 3.) *Kaizen* denotes the importance of the knowledge, skill and experience an individual worker has acquired in their work-role. Who, therefore, is better placed to give advice, set standards for the job? If you want to know about a particular job ask the job holder (*see* Chapter 9 for more on 'kaizen').

There is nothing particularly new here — one hopes that in drawing up job descriptions, for example, you would consult present incumbents. What is new is that the incumbent should be given responsibility for drawing up their *own* description — that this should not be left to so-called experts who in the end will probably evolve a document that reflects the value of *the* management.

It is notable that two of our case studies, **Torquay Leisure Hotel Group** and **Pleasureland**, in drawing up standards from scratch, have *started* by encouraging staff themselves to arrive at their own standards. **Torquay Leisure Hotel Group** has gone one stage further. In selected departments members of staff:

- describe how they carry out a particular task at the moment
- ask themselves *if there are ways in which they can improve on what they do*
- agree with each other how the standard should be described.

Notice the words in italics. This is also part of the *kaizen* concept, not only does the current job-holder know how to do the task they probably could also tell you how it could be done better or differently. So, as you put your standards manual together, why not use the opportunity to review whether you might not change procedures (*see* Chapter 3).

It will not have escaped your notice that emphasis in the above paragraphs tends to be placed on 'management'. This follows the Drucker MBO approach which also became transferred to the process of appraisal itself which tends to be aimed at managers down, perhaps, to supervisors. It should be said that most of our case studies have an appraisal system for managers and supervisors. Nevertheless they are in a transition process of extending it to all staff. **Butlins Southcoast World** does have an elaborate performance review scheme for all staff, as we saw in Chapter 3, based around the Five Star programme. **Pleasureland** also has a performance review for all seasonal staff (Figure 7.2). But these schemes are still *qualitatively* different for those that apply to managers.

While accepting that the *range* and *content* of responsibilities and accountabilities for managers will be different from those of operational staff, we would like to think you could evolve a system of appraisal, part of which is the same for every level of staff. This will also better prepare you for the future and what Handy calls *The Age of Unreason*[6] in which 'everyone will increasingly be expected not only to be good at something, to have their own professional or technical expertise but will also very rapidly acquire responsibility for money, people or property, or all three, a managerial task in fact'.

In the future everyone will be and *should be* managing something or somebody so why not begin to look at the management component of everybody's tasks.[7]

Step 2

Having, ideally, encouraged every member of staff to work with others in agreeing and describing standards of performance, you are now in a much stronger position to introduce systems of review whereby you, as their manager, review with them how well they are meeting these standards and agree action needed to improve or change procedures as necessary. No longer is it *management* imposing a system from on high — it is an opportunity for staff to review their own strengths and weaknesses, and identify what help *they* need to improve. At the same time why not encourage them to appraise you? — it's called 'upward appraisal'![8,9]

You must be careful not to overload the appraisal interview or more properly *discussion*.[10] 'Traditional performance appraisal schemes try to do too much: to set work objectives; to assess work performance for salary purposes; to improve the performance of individuals.'[11] The Nuffield Hospitals Group decided that its appraisals would concentrate on just one goal, personal development. But the trend is to use appraisals for both staff development *and* to review staff performance and set new objectives. What is agreed is that decisions about pay should follow on from agreed results of the appraisal and not be part of it,[11] (For a good text on the process of carrying out appraisal see Fletcher (1993)).

In terms of emphasis on personal development, the Nuffield Hospital scheme poses some useful and essentially straightforward questions for both subordinate and manager to consider. These are summarised on the left in Figure 7.1, while on the right is a summary of the nine topics covered during the discussion.

Questions for subordinate and manager

1. What have I done particularly well at work in the past year?

2. What have I done not so well?

3. What obstacles have I met?

4. What important abilities are not being used?

5. In what aspects of my job do I need more experience and training?

6. To help my personal development, what additional things might be done by:
   (a) My manager? (b) Myself?
   (c) The company?

7. Development actions agreed:
   (a) By me. (b) By my manager.

8. What should I like to be doing in the future?

Order of topics covered in discussion

1. Praise for special achievements.

2. Subordinate's assessment of their own performance.

3. Manager's response to subordinate's assessment.

4. Action to improve subordinate's performance.

5. Subordinate's assessment of the manager.

6. Action to improve manager's performance.

7. Subordinate's career ambitions.

8. Action to achieve subordinate's career ambitions.

9. Summary of actions.

Figure 7.1 Personal development questions in the Nuffield Hospital scheme

Examples of appraisal forms used by our case studies (see below) reflect a number of the principles illustrated in Figure 7.1. Fundamental to all their approaches is that appraisal is only as good as the self-appraisal the individual member of staff is able to undertake for themselves *beforehand*. The appraisal review itself is then simply an opportunity for the manager to respond to the individual's self-assessment and for both of them to agree on level of performance achieved and action for the future. But all this presupposes each manager has been *trained* beforehand to carry out such a review with their staff.

All too often Personnel Departments design the appraisal form and managers are expected to use it without any training. No one appraisal should take place until *all* managers have been trained.[10] If you train your managers to follow the approach illustrated in Figure 7.1 and give them feedback on *the manner* in which they appraise, you will be well on the way to create the culture which we examine in Step 3.

Traditionally two documents have been useful at appraisals—the individual's job description, particularly if it lists what the individual is accountable for, and the previous appraisal which should have summarised objectives and action to be achieved in the next period under review (usually a year but could be less). The action should include what plans are being made for training and developing the member of staff in that period. The outcomes of all the appraisals then gives you your company-wide development plan (*see* Chapter 6).

It also allows you at a subsequent appraisal to *evaluate* the effectiveness of the development that has taken place since the last review. This, I suggest, is the proper time and place for evaluation of training — carried out by the manager and relating *inputs* of training/ development (including review of methods and cost) to *outputs* (what has an individual achieved in performance terms as a consequence of this development). There should be separate provision on the appraisal form for the manager to make this evaluation. This will also enable you to go some way towards meeting the following criteria from Investor in People, which relate to evaluation:

4.1. The organisation evaluates how its development of people is contributing to business goals and targets.

4.2. The organisation evaluates whether its development actions have achieved their objectives.

4.3. The outcomes of training and development are evaluated at individual, team and organisation levels.

4.4. Top management understand the broad costs and benefits of developing people.

4.5 The continuing commitment of top management to developing people is communicated to all employees.

The result of carrying out individual appraisals for *all* members of your staff will provide you with detailed information about every individual and result in a specific action and development programme for each person. But the criteria above require more than simply having the means of collecting evaluative data — they require the organisation to stand back and ask itself what value has been added to the organisation *as a whole* as a result of this development. In my view this is where organisations fall down. They have the individual data but there is one more step required in converting individual results into what has been called 'corporate capability'.[13]

Step 3: Evaluating performance at level of organisation

In addition to having an individual's job description and last appraisal form as you evaluate each member of your staff's performance you should also have in front of you last year's Company Development Plan — with an estimate of costs to be incurred. As you review each member of staff, including the development they've received, you should be building up a picture in your mind of how all of the development that has taken place *adds up*. What is its cumulative effect on the company as a whole? This is essentially what all the Investor in People criterion 4 indicators are asking you to review (*see* Chapter 10).

When you come to the Action Plan you will complete a statement about your view from the top of how value has been added to the organisation as a whole from all these separate individual developments. I call evaluation 'the hidden accumulator' in the sense that if an organisation is evaluating performance at every level it can compile a total picture which is an accumulation of such value.[13] I would argue that in the very *process* of putting this picture together you are adding yet more value. In the final analysis 'Evaluation is the process whereby the organisation is able to see its own image, learn from it and identify the potential for change in the future'.[13] This is crucial to your becoming a *learning organisation* (*see* Conclusions section). In the Action Plan you begin to create a system not only for appraising individuals' performance but also for capturing the learning inherent within the organisation. The final step is then to *communicate* what has been achieved to all employees (*see* Investor in People criteria 4 and 5 and Chapter 9).

The **Oasis** was the first leisure centre to get BS5750 for systems which clearly ensure quality. *But*, in the words of a Senior Manager, 'we are guilty of not saying what we've achieved'. It is often the case that we get so locked *into* the system that we lose sight of its purpose and even more so of the *changes* that the system has brought about. The process of communicating the *results* of evaluation and what has been learned from it is critical. But first let us review how our case studies are using appraisal systems to capture such learning.

7.4 Examples of good practice

A number of references have been made to the Investor in People scheme in this chapter. As the three case studies that have been awarded IiP have found, the development of an appraisal scheme that encompasses all members of staff is central to the whole strategy. It is not surprising therefore that **Butlins Southcoast World**, **Torquay Leisure Hotels** and **Pleasureland** have invested much time in evolving appraisal schemes appropriate to their different cultures. They also build in regular reviews specifically devoted to review of outcomes from *training*. At **Torquay Leisure Hotels**, for example, the MD meets every six months with his General Managers specifically to review training.

In Chapter 3 we have already featured the way **Butlins Southcoast World** links very specific performance measures for staff to NVQ competences. We have already observed that as a result of the way appraisal systems have evolved (through 'Management by Objectives') the focus has inevitably been on managers but all of our case studies recognise the need to extend the process to all staff. In Figure 7.2 we reproduce the simple 'Seasonal Employment Review' used by **Pleasureland** for all of its seasonal staff.

In contrast the company has gone to great lengths to prepare its full-time staff for their annual appraisal. Figure 7.3 is a copy of the introduction sheet all full-time staff get prior to appraisal.

The company puts great emphasis on the need for each staff member to have carried out a 'performance review' *prior* to the appraisal with their boss. It has kept this as open as possible by asking each staff member to respond to the questions as shown in Figure 7.4 on a single sheet.

The focus is on allowing the individual to open up as much as possible. In addition managers are asked to review their specific management role against nationally agreed management occupational standards (as defined by Lead Body MCI) and rate themselves accordingly. As a result of the discussion with their manager, staff agree a rating. But emphasis is on what can be done in future — each member of full-time staff has an individual development plan which identifies objectives to be achieved and a strategy for achieving them.

SEASONAL EMPLOYMENT REVIEW

Manager/Supervisor to complete when reviewing Job Holder's employment six weeks after commence of seasonal employment.

Job Holders Name .... Start Date ....

Current position ....

Manager/Supervisor carrying out review ....

Section A

	GOOD	ACCEPTABLE	POOR
1. Timekeeping			
2. Appearance			
3. Customer Care/Attitude			
4. On Job knowledge			
5. Induction Training Knowledge			
6. Health and Safety Awareness			
7. Initiative			

Section B

Further Training and support needed? (Detail to be given)

Section C

Training/Support outlined in Section B (Give details here of who is to provide, when advised and when training is to be carried out.)

Section D

Please summarise here what has been achieved and also what has been performed well

The above is a true representation of my employment. I also confirm that a 'Job Description' has been issued to me.

Signed .... (Job Holder)   Date ....

Signed .... (Manager/Supervisor)   Date ....

Next Review date (if applicable) ....

Figure 7.2 Pleasureland's seasonal employment review

APPRAISALS

- and how to get the best out of them...

What is an appraisal?

The ultimate purpose of the Appraisal system within Pleasureland is to improve the current and future job performance of each individual and thereby the performance of the Company.

What is the assessment based on?

An assessment is based on set criteria, such as your job description. Your past performance and objectives will be reviewed and your strengths and weaknesses will be discussed in order to highlight any training needs.

Can you fail?

There is no pass or fail with an appraisal. It is merely a discussion and agreement of standards of performance. You may agree that there is a consistently high standard in some areas of your job yet in others, there may be a need to improve. This is not regarded as failing - most people will have some areas in which they wish to improve. An appraisal should be seen as YOUR OPPORTUNITY to discuss YOUR job and your needs. It gives the Management at Pleasureland a clear idea of where you, as an individual, fit into the Company and also enables them to receive feedback to improve YOUR job, job skills and working environment.

Will my potential be realised?

Yes, appraisals look to the future as well as reviewing past performance. Identifying potential is an essential part of the appraisal process.

Will training be provided?

Yes, appraisals look at how to develop potential as well as any weak areas which you have identified. There are plenty of ways to help you develop, for example:-

* A placement in another department to widen your knowledge.

* On the job training from your manager.

* Attending a training course.

During the appraisal, you will have the opportunity to discuss your training needs and solutions, and to plan your year ahead with your Appraiser. You can then both make sure you put the plans into action.

Is it recorded?

Yes, your appraisal form will be written up to record your performance and plans for the following year. You will then be able to add any further comments and sign the appraisal. You can even have a copy if you feel it would be useful to help you follow up on key tasks and training plans or to remind yourself of which areas you want to work on. Shortly after your Appraisal, you will be issued with a Personal Development Plan, which will list any objectives which were agreed during your Appraisal interview. This form will also confirm the date of your next review (if less than 12 months).

So what do I need to do now?

Your manager will let you know the planned date and time of your appraisal. You should prepare by assessing yourself using the PERFORMANCE REVIEW FORM given to you. Try to think of examples of when you have performed well and examples of when you have not done so well. This will form a good basis for a two way discussion with your manager.

And to recap...

1. Use the Performance Review form to prompt your memory for how you have performed since your last Appraisal (or since you began working for this company if this is your first Appraisal).

2. Discuss and reach an agreement about your performance and your future.

3. Outcome - your Personal Development Plan and your key objectives for the next year.

4. Following up on how much you have achieved regularly throughout the year.

Figure 7.3 Pleasureland's appraisal introduction sheet

1. Remind yourself of your key tasks/objectives over the past year and ask yourself how you feel you performed these tasks.

2. What have you found most satisfying this past year?

3. Was there any task which you found most difficult to complete?

4. What do you consider to be your key objectives for this forthcoming year?

5. In which areas do you feel that you may need to develop your knowledge and skills to do your job more efficiently?

6. What activities do you feel would help you to develop these areas (on or off job training for example)?

7. How do you consider you wish your career to develop?

8. Any other comments or thoughts that you would like the opportunity to discuss with your appraiser. (Continue on another sheet if necessary.)

Figure 7.4 Pleasureland's pre-appraisal review questions

At **Beaulieu** the format of the appraisal is very much in line with its culture. Its focus — like **Pleasureland** — is on the *capabilities* of the individual. Figure 7.5 summarises a list of the questions that the appraisee has to complete before the appraisal.

1. Are your duties and responsibilities clear to you?

2. Which of these have been of the most importance since your last appraisal?

3. If you were recruiting the ideal person to take your place what would you look for?

4. To what extent do you match up to these requirements?

5. What is it about your work that gives you the most satisfaction?

6. What do you like least about your job?

7. What achievements are you the most proud of?

8. What goals do you feel you failed to meet?

9. What could you change to improve your performance?

10. What new goals can you establish for the next appraisal period?

11. Is there anything that your supervisor or the organisation does to hinder your effectiveness? If so, what can be done to solve the problem?

12. Does your job make the best of your capabilities? How could you be more effectively used?

13. Do you need any more experience or training to work with increased effectiveness?

14. What do you expect to be doing in five years time?

Figure 7.5 Questions for self-assessment at Beaulieu

We particularly like questions 3 and 4 which help the individual probe quite deeply into the nature of the role and how well they are succeeding in it. Also question 12 which focuses on 'capability' not being used. The Head of Department completes a rather different form which focuses on past and present performance but which also asks, 'Are there any skills or abilities the appraisee possesses which are not utilised by the job? If so could the company make use of them?'

The Personnel Manager looks through every one, particularly to spot opportunities for facilitating a career development. For example, if someone comments, 'I really like meeting people but don't get the chance', the Personnel Manager will look for a vacancy in a more appropriate role. It is this mixing and matching of individual talent that characterises the appraisal process at **Beaulieu**.

In preparing for Investor in People, the **Oasis** Leisure Centre appreciates it has to extend its existing appraisal scheme for managers and supervisors to all staff. Its scheme, like the others we have discussed, gives maximum opportunity for the appraisee to prepare for the appraisal interview, and has prepared guidelines for appraisees to work through before the interview. Four times a year the Centre Manager meets with supervisors to agree, revise targets as necessary and review performance to-date.

Bolton Health Studio is also considering applying for Investor in People. At present it doesn't have a formal Appraisal scheme but what it does have are very clear targets for instructors to achieve — aiming at retaining existing customers. It also has a culture which is very supportive of individual initiative. It therefore meets the two principles we started off with and should have no problem devising a scheme that matches its goals and culture.

7.5 Lessons to be learned

1.   All the companies that have received the Investor in People Award recognise the central importance of having clear standards of performance set for every level of occupation against which staff are regularly reviewed.

2.   Equally the companies recognise the importance of enabling staff to take ownership for determining their own standards of performance and for carrying out a process of *self* appraisal prior to their performance review with their boss.

105

7.6 Action plan

1. Try this experiment. Select three people who undertake three different roles/functions undertaken at your establishment. One function should be a management role, one an administrative role and the third an operational/customer service function. Ask each person to do the following:

    (a) Write down up to three ways in which you would measure success in your job.
    (b) Does your boss assess your performance according to the same criteria?
    (c) How does your boss evaluate your performance?
    (d) When was the last time such evaluation took place?
    (e) When was the last occasion you got any feedback about your performance?

2. Now ask the respective supervisors/managers of these three people these related questions:

    (1) Write down up to three ways in which you would measure the success of respective subordinate.
    (2) How do you evaluate their performance?
    (3) When was the last time you evaluated their performance?
    (4) When was the last time you gave them any feedback about their performance?

3. This step is optional! Ask the same five questions of your own role and compare your answers with your boss's response to the four questions above.

4. Now compare the results from Action points 1 and 2 with the 'company' view as documented in respective job descriptions, appraisal forms (if available). You should find this a salutary exercise. The likelihood is that there would be more data from managers than for the other two roles but also likely that in all three cases there is quite a divergence in the way *individuals* see and measure themselves at work and the company view. One of the themes of this book is to integrate the two views.

    If you have a company where there is complete unity of view between the individual's perception of their job, their bosses' and the company, you are to be congratulated and need not proceed with the rest of this Action Plan. If this exercise has thrown up a number of discrepancies and has made you question existing procedures for describing and evaluating jobs, then we suggest you follow through the rest of the plan and write up in your log.

    The objective is that you avoid the mistake of many companies in rushing to develop new appraisal systems without first involving the very people who will be expected to operate them. Like everything else we've reviewed so far, if you want your staff to own HRM *they* have got to design the systems, not you.

5. The first step is to ensure every job has clearly defined targets. What you did at the end of Chapter 3 should help here by focusing on outcomes and competences. But you may need to be more specific to arrive at least *three* key targets that each person is responsible for. Now define precisely *how* these targets are to be measured.

6. You will also need to take account of your mission and the strategy you have evolved for realising it (*see* Chapter 1). Part of this strategy may have been to set the kinds of targets **Oasis** set for individuals in its Service Plan (*see* Figure 1.2 in Chapter 1). All the time you must balance the targets set for individuals with those set for the organisation as a whole. In this way, when you come to developing a system for appraisal the evaluation of individual targets will have an impact on the organisation as a whole. There is also a need to assess group performance. (NB Investor in People indicator 4.3,

'The outcomes of training and development are evaluated at individual, *team* and organisation levels'.) The following steps suggest a way of arriving at a group consensus about targets as well as ways of reviewing the ways roles are defined and identifying ways of improving. Remember *kaizen*!

7. From your organisation chart (or whatever 'picture' you evolved at the end of Chapter 1), identify the various functional groups/teams that make up your organisation. Get each functional 'head' or supervisor, to ask each member of their team to first write down their response, *individually*, to the following eight questions:

    (a) What do you understand the mission and goals of this organisation to be?
    (b) How do you get information about how well it is being achieved?
    (c) How does the role you perform contribute to the goals of the organisation?
    (d) How do you measure how effective you are in your role?
    (e) How do you get feedback about your own performance?
    (f) What else could you be doing (that you don't or can't do at the moment) that would ensure your role made a more effective contribution?
    (g) What training/development have you had that in your opinion has helped you most to do your job?
    (h) What further training/development/experience do you think you need in future to ensure you make maximum contribution to organisation's goals?

8. Now get the group to share their responses and with the team leader agree what are the critical areas and how they should be assessed.

9. Now get the group to compile their own 'self-assessment review' sheet which reflects the key targets agreed (in response to questions 1–3 and 6), how they should be measured and assessed (questions 4–5) and opportunity for identifying future development needs (7–8). Your team leaders might want to see examples of appraisal forms in Figures 7.1–7.5 for incorporation of particularly revealing questions. Each team leader agrees with team members that this is the basis on which the performance of each of them will be assessed. At the same time they might take the opportunity of agreeing with the team how *they* would judge the leader's performance. (These critical areas would then be brought forward when the team leader has to answer the same eight questions as part of their team — which might be the Heads of Department team meeting under leadership of the General Manager, for example.)

    Another outcome of this kind of process could be a statement from the group as to what are their *team* targets to be met. In this way you can demonstrate how you are evaluating change not just of individuals but of groups. It also provides you with targets that can be rewarded in specific ways thus giving incentives to everyone to perform well not just individually but as members of teams (*see* Chapter 9)

10. After you have got back responses from all the teams (including the one that you directly manage — possibly the Heads of Department group) you will be in a position to compile an assessment form that reflects company-wide practice. It maybe that as General Manager there are additional areas you would wish to see reflected on the form — if so these will have to be negotiated through the team mechanism described above.

11. As a result of following through the above steps you should now be able to carry out the exercise with which we started (Action plan points 1–4) and, hopefully, arrive at a very different result — one of a consensus of assessors and assessed, an integration of the needs of the individual with the team, and ultimately of the company.

12. In the final analysis only you, as senior manager, can put the total company-wide picture together. Only you can recognise what is the added value for the company as a whole. We suggest that this is a combined *value* of the extent to which mission and core values from Chapter 1 have been realised and the 'accumulator' effect of adding together individual and group performance derived from the process we have described above.

The results of *your* evaluation should then be shared with every member of your staff. Why not incorporate it into your annual report or include it regularly once a year in the monthly newsletter (*see* Chapter 9). By incorporating details of the outcome of training and development (which are *not* separate but part of overall evaluation) you will also be meeting Investors in People criterion indicator 4.5: 'Training success and major achievements will be publicised as a matter of course — because they are seen as important … Where training and development has contributed to business success this fact should be fully recognised.'

In Chapter 8 we look at ways you can 'recognise' and reward this achievement.

7.7 References

1. Armstrong, M. (1992) *Human Resource Management — Strategy and Action* p. 162, Kogan.

2. Kearns, P. and Miller, M. (1993) The financial return for training and development: hard facts or act of faith? *Transition*, Vol. 93, Issue 9, October 1993.

3. Hamblin, A. C. (1974) *Evaluation and Control of Training* McGraw Hill.

4. Herzberg, F., Mausner, B. and Synderman, B. (1959) *The Motivation to Work* John Wiley.

5. Drucker, P. (1954) *The Practice of Management* Harper and Row.

6. Handy, C. (1989) *The Age of Unreason* Hutchinson.

7. Willie, E. (1990) Should management development just be for managers? *Personnel Management* August 1990.

8. Hall, H. (1992) Open to criticism *Personnel Today* 21 April–4 May 1992, p. 3 1

9. Fletcher, C. (1993) Appraisal: an idea whose time has gone? *Personnel Management* September 1993.

10. Fowler, A. (1991) How to conduct appraisals *Personnel Management Plus* Vol. 2, No. 6, June 1991, pp. 22–23.

11. Wilson, J. and Cole, Graham. (1990) A healthy approach to performance appraisal *Personnel Management* June 1990, pp. 46–49.

12. Fletcher, C. (1993) *Appraisal: routes to improved performance* IPM.

13. Critten, P. (1993) *Investing in People: Towards Corporate Capability* Butterworth Heinemann.

14. Neale, F. (Ed) (1992) *The Handbook of Performance Management* IPM.

15. Fletcher, C. and Williams, R. (1992) The route to performance management *Personnel Management* October 1992.

8. *Paying for performance and reward management*

8.1 The principles

Just as jobs and the nature of work have undergone wide-ranging changes so too has the whole concept of pay and how people are rewarded at work. The following description reflects the way most organisations in the past have gone about determining how to remunerate staff:

> *Traditional organisations typically create fixed jobs with a clearly defined purpose, accountabilities and competency requirements. They use job evaluation to rank jobs in terms of their perceived importance to the organisation. They use job size to determine basic pay levels by referring to comparative practice in the external pay market. They select individuals to fill each job by assessing the fit of their competencies with job requirements. They then pay individuals by assessing the relative level of their experience and performance against the requirements of the job.[1]*

This statement also reflects a number of cultural assumptions and values from the past such as, equity, equal pay for work of equal value, hierarchy, control and permanently defined jobs. These were the circumstances that prevailed in the 1960s and 1970s when many organisations first introduced job evaluation. The focus was very much on jobs rather than people and this is the rationale for job evaluation. It is a process for giving a ranking to one job as compared with another in the same organisation in terms of its size and importance taking account of a range of factors (e.g. accountability, initiative, resources control, supervision given/received).

This is not the place to give a detailed account of job evaluation, for that *see* Murlis and Fitt (1991) and Fowler (1992), but merely to note its importance in the past in determining the wage bands within which groups of jobs within an organisation would fall.[3] Most salaried employees (i.e. not hourly paid) would recognise that on joining a company they would be assigned a particular point on a wage scale and that there would be so many 'increments' on this scale. The company would set down conditions for moving from one to another. This might be simply being in a job for a period of time (though it might now be linked to the kind of performance factors we discussed in the previous chapter). Once you reached 'the top of the scale' the only way of getting more money meant you had to get another job (which usually meant some form of promotion) as a result of which you fell into another scale and so on.

So what has changed? In the 1980s there was an increasing move away from national pay bargaining to local agreements putting pressure on individual companies to devise their own pay structures. Also, as we have observed on more than one occasion in this book, external markets were becoming more volatile and the *performance* of individuals inside the company was becoming more of a critical issue than the *job* they were undertaking.

> *Alongside these developments, the 1980s also saw radical changes in the way businesses are structured and organised, with the emergence of flatter, more*

> *fluid organisations and greater reliance on teamwork and flexibility. The concept of a job as a nice neat box on an organisation chart no longer reflects the reality of the way most organisations work. Inevitably the validity of conventional job evaluation techniques in these circumstances is questioned.*[4]

The first principle is that increasingly organisations are looking for ways of rewarding individual and team performance as opposed to merely paying the market-rate for a job. So-called performance related pay (PRP) is also very much in the news as social services like the police, teachers and nurses become very anxious about individual targets taking over from the core service they are expected to provide. There has also been much debate about how effective PRP has been amongst HRM professionals themselves with mixed results.

In 1991 a major research project by IPM into performance management and PRP concluded from responses from 1,000 organisations that three-quarters of them had some form of PRP but that poor financial performers were equally likely to have PRP as good performers.[5] An ACAS report is critical of an underlying assumption of PRP that everything is measurable.[6] But most reports also agree that PRP *is* effective if it is part of a *strategic* approach based on a well-defined performance management system (*see* Chapter 7).[7]

As with other initiatives we have discussed, e.g. competences and NVQs, what is at issue very often is the *way* they are introduced not the principle itself. The principle we adhere to in this chapter is that the leisure industry, like most other industries, must find its *own* way of rewarding staff based on clear performance criteria. But underlying this is another much deeper principle which is at the heart of all reward management — motivation.

Performance related pay is usually linked with one particular school of motivation called 'expectancy theory'.[8] This indicates that pay is only part of what is a complex of *perceptions* a given individual has about what is an appropriate reward for themselves in relation to a given amount of effort. There are two types of reward — *extrinsic* (supplied by the organisation) and *intrinsic* (motivations within the individual). You may or may not be someone who is so absorbed by the work that you do that you often work beyond hours expected of you for no additional *extrinsic* reward other than realising personal (i.e. intrinsic) satisfaction. Even if you wouldn't agree with such a principle, I'm sure you can recognise it in others!

You should also be aware of the findings of another key survey that has ever since had implications for HRM, that of Frederick Herzberg who in the 1950s posed two questions to a number of employees (notably professionals):

> *When you are satisfied at work, what is making you happy?*

> *When you are dissatisfied at work, what is making you unhappy?*

As a result of their responses he propounded his Two-Factor theory of motivation.[9] On the one hand there were *hygiene* factors (tend to be *extrinsic*, wages, working conditions, company policy, supervision and interpersonal relations); on the other hand there were *motivators* (*intrinsic* factors such as achievement, recognition, responsibility and advancement). What he found was that hygiene factors (pay etc.) ensured that employees were not *dissatisfied*. But this did not necessarily mean that this was sufficient to motivate them. To be motivated the organisation needed to ensure that every employee was able to realise *motivators* like recognition and responsibility.

Critics of Herzberg are concerned that he interviewed only professionals (engineers and accountants), that people will naturally ascribe unfavourable events to causes outside themselves, that not *everyone* is motivated by intrinsic drives — these are just some of the criticisms. *However*, most surveys about what motivate employees at work seem to reinforce the findings, notably that pay is, contrary to popular belief, *not* necessarily a motivator. On the other hand people *are* motivated by responsibility, empowerment and, more and more, by opportunities for self-development and recognition.

So, where does all this get us? The second principle is that there can never be one universal system of reward that is appropriate to all companies.

> *Every organisation has to work out its own reward philosophy in the light of the analysis of business and individual needs. Philosophies are therefore contingent upon the organisation's strategy, culture and values, and on the type of people it employs.*[10]

Principle 1 focused on *performance* in a job rather than rewarding the job itself. Principle 2 extends reward philosophy to encompass the kind of *skills* the organisation wishes to encourage. In an influential book on the *strategic* aspects of pay, E Lawler III argues that organisations should go beyond paying people for the job they do and 'offer incentives that clearly develop the skills that will give the organisation a competitive advantage in the market place'.[11] Payment for skills and competences could mean that somebody lower in the job hierarchy could earn more than their boss!

Lawler even foresees the ultimate in a 'participative approach to pay', whereby individuals decide their own base pay and what incentives and bonus they should receive! This may seem to you inconceivable but the principle to take on board is that the way you reward staff (and, indeed, how clearly you *communicate* that policy) says a lot about the company you are and can be a very powerful source of change. (*See* Hall (1993), which describes a Brazilian company where workers *do* determine their own pay.) We will look at what options are available to you in section 8.3 but to end this preliminary section consider how Ros Moss Kanter sees the pay check of the future: 'As many as five variables will determine the final numbers: for example,

1. A guaranteed small base amount based on organisational level and position.

2. Individual merit component.

3. Group or division gain-sharing component.

4. Overall company-profit sharing component.

5. From time to time one-shot, short-term bonuses and recognition awards for exemplary individual and team contributions.'[12]

Clearly management information systems will need to get a lot more sophisticated to handle this complexity, but in the meantime you might consider how more flexible your reward system could be and to what extent it meets the above principles.

8.2 What's in it for me?

1. Being clear about exactly what it is you are rewarding (e.g. performance/skills) enables you better to focus on key result areas and ensure that people take ownership for their performance *and* development .

2. A more cost-effective way of allocating resources.

3. To pay and reward people in accordance with their contribution is in line with the equitable strategy you arrived at in Chapter 2.

4. A clear reward strategy related to contribution signals a message to all employees as to the kind of culture to which they belong and puts pressure on them to identify with it (or to leave). Obversely it will attract to you the kind of high quality staff you need.

8.3 What's involved?

The first step is to be clear about what your *current* policy for paying and rewarding staff is.

- Is base pay determined by job evaluation and/or what the market will pay for a given job?
- Do you pay over the market rate as an incentive?
- How many pay scales do you have and what is the basis for determining incremental points on the scale?
- Is there a different rate of pay for part-time or seasonal staff?
- Over and above base pay can individuals get incentive pay?
- Over and above base pay, can individuals share in bonuses allocated by the company? On what basis are such bonuses paid?
- Can individuals get a pay incentive on demonstrating competence, reaching a particular standard, being awarded a qualification (e.g. NVQ)?
- What non-financial incentives are there for staff? (e.g. discount on meals, goods, use of facilities, vouchers to buy goods, prizes?

Answers to these questions will give you an idea about the current remuneration strategy of your company.

You should also recognise that under the law, discussed fully in Chapter 2, employees have some basic rates in relation to pay. With the abolition of the Wages Council in 1993 there is no longer a minimum wage but individuals have a number of rights under the following laws:

1. As a result of The Wages Act (1986) the method of paying wages is *now a matter for agreement* between employer and employee and *deductions* from wages may not be made unless it is authorised by statute or by a relevant provision of the employee's contract or by the employee himself in advance in writing.

2. Under the Employment Protection (Consolidated) Act (1978) an employee with more than one month's continuous service is entitled to a *guarantee payment* for up to five days in any period of three months for days when they would not normally be expected to work but no work is available for them.

3. Under the same Act (EP(C)A) each employee is entitled to an *itemised pay statement* which must show gross pay and take-home pay, with amounts and reasons for all fixed and variable deductions.

The next question to ask is: is this strategy appropriate to your mission (Chapter 1), with the kind of roles and competences you want to develop (Chapter 3) and finally, does it allow you to recognise sufficiently the performance of staff when you come to appraise them (Chapter 7)? Only you can say what is appropriate for your company and its strategy for the future. Below are some notes about the various kinds of reward packages available to you. Armstrong and Murtis (1991) is a useful source for reference.

Determining base rates of pay

As we have discussed, traditionally this done by job evaluation. This involves the following stages:[3]

1. Job ranking: each job is ranked accordingto a range of factors (e.g. accountability, initiative, resources control, supervision given/received) that differentiate one job from another.

2. Job grouping: according to ranks assigned, jobs are now grouped into salary scales.

3. Scale differentials: this will depend on the number of scales — the fewer the scales the larger the differentials between scales (i.e. difference between minima of adjacent scales).

4. Scale width: this is the percentage by which the maximum of a scale exceeds the minimum. If fixed increments are to be given you might want a narrow scale; on the other hand if salary progression is to be based on performance assessments you may want wider spans. The mid-point of a scale is usually the point of comparison with rates paid in the market.

5. Setting values on scales: finally, this pitches the respective salary scales at appropriate levels in comparison with similar jobs in the market place. But depending on your plans for the future and the mix of other benefits that will make up the final reward package — this may be higher or lower than salaries paid by the market for similar jobs.

The base rate of pay is the most usual way of rewarding staff — but it is often not clear on what basis an individual moves up the scale. As we have seen there is a move away from giving 'fixed increments' to linking *differentials* in pay with clear performance criteria. Performance related pay covers a wide spectrum. First, let us be clear how it is defined:

Performance-related pay is that part of the financial, or financially measurable, reward to an individual which is linked directly to individual, team or company performance.[7]

Let us look at types of reward that fit into these three categories.

Individual PRP

Merit pay
Of all PRP schemes this is the one that is part of the base salary structure; it is the basis on which a base salary increase is paid in relation to specified performance criteria. Thus if two people are on the same incremental point of scale and one's performance is judged 'outstanding' while other is 'below average' — one would receive an agreed merit rise while other may or may not receive any merit rise.

Individual bonuses
These come from cash sums that are *separate* from those budgeted to pay base salaries and merit increases. It has usually applied to senior managers and sales staff who achieve specifically measurable outputs (profits/sales/increase in customers).

Whatever level of staff is targeted it is important that the achievement of the objective is wholly within their control. (*See* Chapter 10 for setting objectives in a participative way.)

The 'bonus pool' from which awards are made is generated by the performance for which an agreed proportion of that bonus is given (e.g. sales staff at **Bolton Health Studio** get an individual bonus in proportion to their contributing to increased revenue from membership of new clients).

Group/team bonus

As we have discovered, there is an increasing emphasis on rewarding *team* performance. Again the bonus pool comes from increases in revenue in a particular area but this time the whole group is rewarded, each member receiving the same amount (though it *can* be arranged that different individuals get different amounts depending on their contribution). An example might be that all the team in your cafeteria get together to plan how to increase sales of, say, salads. After a period of time it is found that profit from sales has increased significantly and a proportion of that profit is allocated to be distributed equally amongst the group. Clearly such a scheme encourages team work and group ownership.

It can also be used to target particular problems, like accident rates and absenteeism. BP Oil UK's distribution division has set targets for reducing accidents which also involves peer pressure. Individuals can get £300 or £400 bonus as a member of a team with no accident.[14] But if an individual does have an accident not only do they lose their month's points — so does the team!

Gainsharing

This is a particular type of bonus where what is shared is a measurable 'gain' derived from comparisons with historical data. For example it might be that as a result of the efforts of a group of accounts clerks, debts are cut over a given period. In this case no target was set, but it can be seen that 'productivity' has improved. The 'bonus pool' is calculated according to the proportional gain in getting money from debtors over similar periods in the past.

A famous example of a 'gainsharing' scheme is the 'Scanlon Plans' which began life in the manufacturing industry to give employees a greater say in how their abilities could be used for both the benefit of themselves and the company. It required workers and management representatives to form committees to agree on ways to improve the business — usually derived from suggestions schemes. A bonus payment was made on the basis of positive changes in the ratio of labour cost to the total production value over agreed time period. To some extent there are similarities with 'quality circles' except that members don't necessarily benefit financially.

Company based schemes

Profit Share

Such schemes are not technically PRP in that they don't aim to increase performance (at least directly). But it reflects a level of performance that the company has achieved (usually in terms of profit) a proportion of which is distributed either to all employees (on the basis that collectively they made it happen) or to a designated group. They have become more popular recently because some of them can attract tax advantages for employees. (Inland Revenue requires 80 per cent of staff to be covered in company scheme.)

Share schemes   These enable employees (usually senior managers) to take advantage of share option schemes that allow them to share in the fortunes of the company.

So far we have concentrated on building up a reward package based on *financial* returns. But there are a range of schemes that provide additional incentives not directly linked to money payments.

Cafeteria route to compensation   So-called because it offers a 'menu' of benefits for employees to choose what mix of benefits they want. This is a typical 'menu' of benefits each incurring different costs.[15]

Car	Loans
Pension	Counselling
Life assurance	Childcare vouchers
Disability cover	Retail vouchers
Medical insurance	Dental scheme
Annual leave	Sports clubs
Private petrol	Paid for holidays
Mortgage subsidy	

Fowler (1993) is a useful source for guidelines on the costing of flexible benefits.[16]

Incentive gifts   Less sophisticated but nevertheless just as effective are the range of individual gifts that can indicate that a company values individual performance. This could range from a T-shirt to a holiday in Miami.

Paying for skills

As we saw from the first section there is a move to rewarding people for the skills they have as well as the application of those skills in effective performance. An IPM report indicates that a quarter of employees responding to a joint IPM/NEDO survey said that they had introduced changes to their payment system to encourage the acquisition of new skills.[17] As we shall see when we look at our case studies, this is an area which the leisure industry might look at further; but as the IPM report advises, a company has to be very clear as to what are the skills to be remunerated. Simply attending a training course would not be sufficient — there would also have to be evidence that an individual can *apply* these skills resulting in an NVQ, for example (*see* Chapters 3 and 6).

We have now completed a whistle-stop review of the key approaches for compiling a reward management package that meets the principles with which we started. As such it has:

- to reward specific performance which will contribute to individual, team and company goals (*see* Chapter 7)
- to reward the application of specific skills which the organisation wishes to develop (*see* Chapter 3)
- to pay the rate at which such skills are valued in the market.

In such a labour intensive industry as the leisure industry the wages bill is always going to be the highest cost item. As with any other cost it must be carefully budgeted for and monitored. Each organisation will have its own procedure for budgeting for staff costs and monitoring them. The value placed on an organisation's staff is as much a function of an organisation's awareness of how much it costs to employ them as on assessment of their performance.

You should have a system whereby you have at least a monthly summary of gross wage costs budgeted and actual costs incurred. At **Torquay Leisure Hotels**, where operational staff are paid on a two-weekly basis, Heads of Department get a fortnightly statement of gross wages paid in the last two weeks which they can use to check the budget for the next two weeks ensuring that peaks and troughs are accounted for. When the monthly company account figures are received they are better able to check any variations between actual and budgeted figures.

As wage bills become more complex, reflecting the variety of ways in which staff are rewarded (see Ros Moss Kanter's predictions above), the use of personal computers and simple spreadsheet packages are going to be an essential piece of equipment in every leisure manager's office.

8.4 Examples of good practice

Pleasureland, as we saw, has a detailed appraisal scheme for full-time staff which is carried out in December. A salary review takes place in June. Over and above base rates individual staff will be awarded merit increases depending on their performance and perceived value to the company. At Christmas each member of staff gets a share of the profits.

Seasonal staff are hourly paid. There is a plan to recognise the different levels of competence they achieve by an added financial bonus. At the moment recognition comes with the award of a certificate of competence.

Butlins Southcoast World has a similar system. As we saw in Chapters 3 and 6 its Five Star performance scheme is undertaken by all staff — seasonal and full-time. There are plans to link progression up the 5 star system with some form of skills related remuneration.

Bolton Health Studio has two schemes relating to two teams, Sales and Retention, each member of which can get a bonus (over and above hourly rate) by meeting and exceeding set targets. What is interesting is that the Retention Scheme (retention of clients) covers reception and gym instructors. Over a 12-month period they mean to considerably exceed the average 40 per cent retention rate and every team member will be given an equal bonus.

The aim of the studio is to ensure everyone has some target to aim for, even the administration staff. A scheme has been started to target collection of 'arrears'. If a target is met and exceeded a bonus will be given.

In addition, top performers are identified from time to time and rewards could be anything from a dinner for two to a holiday in Miami. In the summer-time months — traditionally a low season for gyms — staff have targets set under 'commit to fitness', encouraging customers to come in and get sponsorship for charity. (For the second year running the studio has won the prize for collecting the most money for charity.)

8.5 Lessons to be learned

It is clear there is no universal reward package. In an industry with such a dependence on seasonal staff it is difficult to have a uniform scheme for full-time, part-time and seasonal staff. But there are some trends to be detected:

1. An increasing emphasis on the setting of clear performance targets — for all staff — which can be appropriately rewarded regardless of the mode of contract.

2. All case studies, not surprisingly, depend very heavily on 'intrinsic' rewards, on the capability of staff to take ownership for their own development. It is interesting in an industry not well known for high rates of pay that it compensates for this by providing an ideal culture for people to acquire multi-skills.

3. An emphasis on rewarding individuals as members of teams.

8.6 Action plan

1. Be clear on what basis staff are paid at the moment and how staff *perceive* they are being paid. Lawler remarks that many a company may have a very elaborate reward package for selected individuals but if they are sworn to secrecy there is no way the organisation culture can benefit as a whole.[14] You might consider carrying out a survey of staff's perceptions of the way they are paid. Are they aware of others' rates of pay? Do they see a clear link between what they do and how they are rewarded (the fundamental principle underpinning 'expectancy theory')? Are they aware of the range of incentives on offer to *everyone?*

2. In your Action Plan you will see a proforma in which you can record the results of your findings. It also includes a proforma to summarise the results of how staff *perceive* the way they are paid.

3. By comparing one set of results with the other, what conclusion do you come to? Write a report detailing your findings and recommendations for an improved reward system. This should indicate:
    — How it contributes to the mission statement (Chapter 1).
    — How it reflects the kind of staff and working practices you wish to introduce in the future (Chapters 2 and 3).
    — How it rewards the development of key skills and competences (Chapter 3).
    — How it meets specific goals set in Chapter 7.

If you read through the Action Plans for the last seven chapters you should have in place an ideal system for investing in people. Before we look in more detail at what is required to meet Investor in People criteria, there are just two more *processes* you should review to ensure the system is embedded most effectively. The first looks at systems for involving all members of staff and the second for ways of communicating effectively. Both are covered in Chapter 9.

8.7 References

1. Murlis, H. and Fitt, D. (1991) Job evaluation in a changing world *Personnel Management* May 1991, pp. 39–43.

2. Fowler, A. (1992) How to choose a job evaluation system *Personnel Management Plus* Vol. 3, No. 10, October 1992, pp. 33–34.

3. Fowler, A. (1990) How to design a salary structure *Personnel Management Plus* Vol. 1, No. 6, December 1990, pp. 20–21.

4. Murlis, H. and Pritchard , D. (1991) The computerised way to evaluate jobs *Personnel Management* April 1991, pp. 48–53.

5. IPM (1992) *Performance Management in the UK: an Analysis of the Issues* IPM.

6. ACAS (1992) *Motivating and Rewarding Employees: Some Aspects of Theory and Practice* ACAS.

7. Wright, V. (1992) Performance-related pay in Neale, F. (Ed) *The Handbook of Performance Management* IPM.

8. Nadler, D. A. and Lawler, E.E. III (1977) Motivation: a diagnostic approach in Hackman, J. R., Lawler, E. III and Protek, L. W. *Perspectives on Behaviour in Organisations* McGraw Hill.

9. Herzberg, F., Mausner, B. and Synderman, B. (1959) *The Motivation to Work* John Wiley.

10. Armstrong, M. (1992) *Human Resource Management: Strategy and Action* Kogan Page.

11. Lawler, E. (1990) *Strategic Pay — Aligning Organizational Strategies and Pay Systems* Jossey Bass p. 23,

12. Kanter, R. M. (1989) *When Giants learn to Dance* Simon and Schuster .

13. Armstrong, M. and Murlis, H. (1991) *Reward Management* Kogan Page.

14. Special report (1993) Fuelling the safety drive *Personnel Today* 4–17 May 1993, p. 23.

15. Woodley, C. (1993) The benefits of flexibility *Personnel Management* May 1993, pp. 36–39.

16. Fowler, A. (1993) How to manage flexible benefits *Personnel Management Plus* Vol. 4, No. 7, July 1993, pp. 23–24.

17. Kimber, E. (1992) *Skills-Based Pay: a Guide for Practitioners* IPM.

18. Hall, L. (1993) The boss from Brazil *Personnel Today* 26 October 1993.

9. Communication and employee involvement

9.1 The principles

It is often said that the best form of communication is a two-way process. One-way communication can never ensure that the message has been understood as intended — there must be some form of feedback loop. In the context of organisations the one-way communication process is the top-down transmission of messages, targets, from management to staff. The feedback loop must come from staff themselves and is a function of how well an organisation encourages the involvement of staff not just to respond to the *management* view but to put forward suggestions of their own. The extent to which organisations use both approaches is the subject of this chapter.

We had intended to write two separate chapters — one on top-down communication and the other on bottom-up involvement. But it soon became clear that the two subjects are (or should be) inextricably intertwined — though this principle is far from being universally applied. In a recent survey of communication practice in 100 public and private sector companies the internal communication consultancy Smythe Dorward Lambert concluded that a mere 5 per cent of companies used internal communication to enable employees to contribute to the changes going on around them.[1]

According to this report, for the majority of companies surveyed communication *is* a one-way process. Most companies still put out information which reinforces the company line while giving low priority to issues raised by staff. Nevertheless the report does cite examples of companies who have dramatically changed their communication policy — usually in response to a lowering in staff morale caused by what is seen as a lowering of employment conditions. Companies like Lloyds Bank have introduced a charter of 15 standards for internal communications in response to employees' criticisms in the past. One standard pledges that it will be open and honest with employees whether the news is good or bad. Also that senior managers will chair local meetings with staff at which they can raise any question. This is similar to a communication campaign launched by Nationwide to encourage local branches to run 'talkback' meetings where again senior managers could be challenged by staff and indeed the proceedings were videoed.[2]

Another survey was carried out in 1989 specifically to look at the extent of employee involvement in 25 organisations of size varying from 50 employees to over 50,000 representing private service, manufacturing and public sector organisations.[3] It identified four main types of employee involvement. These are summarised below with numbers of organisations using particular method indicated in brackets

1. Direct communications (written and face to face):
   — Regular briefing sessions (19).
   — Company newspapers (19).
   — Employee reports (9).

2. Problem solving groups:
   — TQM/customer care (19).

      — Suggestion schemes (15).
      — Attitude surveys (5).
      — Quality circles (5).

3.   Financial employee involvement:
      — Profit sharing/employee share ownership (16).
      — Value added/establishment wide bonuses (5).

4.   Staff representation (often, but not always on basis of union membership):
      — Collective bargaining (17).
      — Joint consultative committees (JCCs) (15).
      — Works councils/directors (2).

A significant finding was that employee involvement schemes were seen as most important in those organisations (mainly manufacturing) who had introduced schemes over a longer period of time. This started with JCCs in the 1970s (reflecting the age of industrial democracy), followed by structured communication devices in the 1980s (reflecting the age of top-down communication and commitment) followed by TQM and problem solving groups (reflecting the age of empowerment of the 1990s).

In contrast there was a second group drawn from service industries in the private sector where a number of different schemes were introduced in a much shorter time-span often leading to confusion and even conflict between one scheme and another. They identified a third group (more typical of smaller organisations) where the schemes were perceived to be the latest fad and fashion and had no significant impact. This leads authors to conclude:

> *Much depends upon the context in which employee involvement is practised, how it is introduced, and the degree to which different schemes are integrated with the strategic objectives of the organisation as a whole'.*[3]

So, yet again, the same theme is apparent — any HRM scheme *must* match an organisation's goals and objectives. There is another allied principle: 'the need for consistency between formal and informal communications modes'.[4] As every manager will know, however much money is spent on the most sophisticated of communication media, the most effective will always be the informal internal and external 'grapevine' — staff gossip, they talk to staff from other establishments, they read newspapers. Instead of ignoring the informal grapevine in favour of more sophisticated and glossy methods of communication, *make-use of it*, make it the centre-piece of your campaign. Remember how John Major turned the tide in the run-up to the election of 1992 by abandoning the formal 'briefing' methods and getting on his 'soap-box' to meet the people. Remember how, ironically, this contrasted with the glitz of Labour's stage-managed 'presentations'.

If you are about to send out a memorandum/circular to staff, you might consider if it wouldn't be better to walk over and discuss the matter with them personally or alternatively you might turn to section 9.3 for a range of options to choose from.

9.2 What's in it for me?

1.   However well you may have followed through the arguments in this book so far and planned to use them in your Action Plan, unless you actually *communicate* them to your staff you will never know how good (or not!) they are.

2. There is no good idea which can't be bettered in discussion with others. You are the catalyst for change but only your staff can make it happen. Your plans are only half the equation — the contribution your staff make *in response* not only complements your proposals they are likely to make them even better.

3. Commitment, particularly commitment to change, has to be owned internally — no amount of *external* exhortation (however attractively packaged) can *of itself* lead to change. Many of the methods we discuss in section 9.3 can help provide information and support for a particular idea, action, but unless an individual is enabled to *own* it as if it was theirs, action won't happen. People support what they help to create.

4. The more open you are with your employees, the more information you give them, the more likely is it that you would meet codes of practice now enshrined in law (*see* Chapter 2) and in particular anticipate likely requirements of EC law (Social Charter or no Charter) by the end of the century.

5. Finally, as we shall see in section 9.3, communication and employee involvement is at the heart of the 'Investor in People' award so that any system of open communication you initiate now will help your case.

9.3 What's involved?

This section is an overview of a range of methods, principles all of which make up good communication practice. They are divided into two — top-down (i.e. management communicating to staff) and bottom-up (methods for involving staff). *But* as we've discussed above they should all be part of one strategy.

Keeping staff informed

Team briefing

Team briefing is a system of communication driven by managers to cascade information down the line so that *all* employees share the same information. It was championed by the Industrial Society in the 1980s which laid down a number of key principles.[5] It usually followed a senior management meeting, was to be given by the manager of a designated group or section (team to comprise between 3–15), to last no more than 30 minutes; there should be no more than four levels in the cascade system from senior management to the shop floor and all employees should be briefed within 48 hours.

As we shall see all our case studies use a form of team briefing, particularly **Swindon Leisure Centre**. But, because of the predominance of shift systems the process has to be adapted to combine 'shift meetings' and the more typical team briefing approach.

In the past there has been some scepticism about the motives of team briefings which are seen to reinforce management's prerogatives (particularly by the unions). However, that may be changing as more companies appreciate the value of *kaizen* with the result that team briefing becomes much more of a two-way communication process. However such meetings are used, everyone is agreed that managers need training in presentation and briefing skills.

Mass meetings

While briefing groups are effective at focusing on specific issues, our case studies also recognise the usefulness of the 'annual meeting' for *all* staff which is partly PR but can also serve as a forum for putting forward the company's mission or strategy which can then be debated separately through other more participative meetings. By its very nature it is a one-way process of communication.

One-to-one meetings
Any meeting between manager and a member of staff can be used to impart information — though it is wise to make a note each time of just what information was communicated to ensure that the message doesn't change and thereby lead to confusion via the grapevine. An appraisal 'discussion' (*see* Chapter 8) is also a good opportunity for reinforcing key messages that as a manager you wish to ensure gets communicated down the line.

Memoranda/circulars
Such methods of communication are often abused and ineffective.How often have you received a memo from a manager which, on the face of it looks exactly the same as one you received last week and so you discard it without further scrutiny or taking any action. It might be that hidden within it was a vital new piece of information which requires urgent action. If you are sending information in this way you must:

1. Be very clear what outcome you want to achieve, i.e. is it just for information or is action required? *Indicate* this clearly at top.

2. If possible have a standard format which separates out background information from details of what needs to be done.

3. Indicate how outcome will be followed up (e.g. at a later meeting etc).

Notice boards
These are even more abused! 'Dull-looking, badly worded typed announcements, pinned carelessly among a clutter of dog-eared and out-of-date notices are not a good way of attracting attention or relaying important messages'.[4] So much so that in some of our case studies staff members had specific responsibility for keeping the notice board up to date. In an industry that depends on shift work, well-placed notice boards can be a valuable source of information *as long as* you make it clear that this is the medium you will use to post important notices. If not why should staff look at it?

In-house journals
Most of our case studies had an in-house staff manual that was published three or four times a year. A typical example from the **Oasis** can be seen in Figure 9.1.

It combines gossip and fun with serious factual issues and news and can be very effective. Also, it was obvious judging by the quality of production of the journals I saw that the organisations took them very seriously.

Annual report
In the same way as in-house journals are becoming more professional and attractively produced so too are annual reports. They are also being aimed as much at staff as at shareholders and clients. In the past they tended to be filled with page after page of text and statistics. Now text is likely to be attractively split up into columns (thanks to desktop publishing) and to be interspersed with photographs (often in colour) and the statistics will use graphics and be user friendly.

Videos and technology
It is becoming more common practice for companies to use videos to get across their messages. Some national and multinational companies use them to record the annual speech

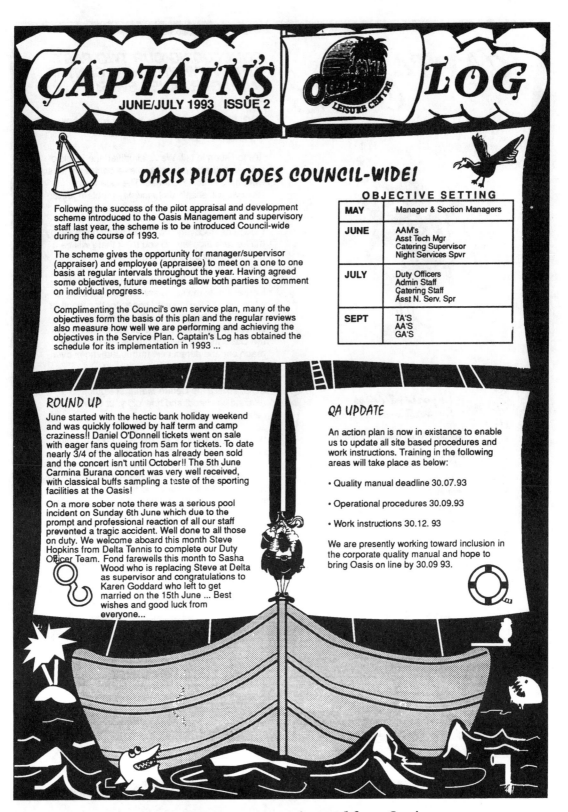

CAPTAIN'S LOG

JUNE/JULY 1993   ISSUE 2

OASIS PILOT GOES COUNCIL-WIDE!

Following the success of the pilot appraisal and development scheme introduced to the Oasis Management and supervisory staff last year, the scheme is to be introduced Council-wide during the course of 1993.

The scheme gives the opportunity for manager/supervisor (appraiser) and employee (appraisee) to meet on a one to one basis at regular intervals throughout the year. Having agreed some objectives, future meetings allow both parties to comment on individual progress.

Complimenting the Council's own service plan, many of the objectives form the basis of this plan and the regular reviews also measure how well we are performing and achieving the objectives in the Service Plan. Captain's Log has obtained the schedule for its implementation in 1993 ...

OBJECTIVE SETTING

MAY	Manager & Section Managers
JUNE	AAM's Asst Tech Mgr Catering Supervisor Night Services Spvr
JULY	Duty Officers Admin Staff Catering Staff Asst N. Serv. Spr
SEPT	TA'S AA'S GA'S

ROUND UP

June started with the hectic bank holiday weekend and was quickly followed by half term and camp craziness!! Daniel O'Donnell tickets went on sale with eager fans queing from 5am for tickets. To date nearly 3/4 of the allocation has already been sold and the concert isn't until October!! The 5th June Carmina Burana concert was very well received, with classical buffs sampling a taste of the sporting facilities at the Oasis!

On a more sober note there was a serious pool incident on Sunday 6th June which due to the prompt and professional reaction of all our staff prevented a tragic accident. Well done to all those on duty. We welcome aboard this month Steve Hopkins from Delta Tennis to complete our Duty Officer Team. Fond farewells this month to Sasha Wood who is replacing Steve at Delta as supervisor and congratulations to Karen Goddard who left to get married on the 15th June ... Best wishes and good luck from everyone...

QA UPDATE

An action plan is now in existance to enable us to update all site based procedures and work instructions. Training in the following areas will take place as below:

• Quality manual deadline 30.07.93

• Operational procedures 30.09.93

• Work instructions 30.12. 93

We are presently working toward inclusion in the corporate quality manual and hope to bring Oasis on line by 30.09 93.

Figure 9.1 In-company journal from Oasis

CAPTAIN'S CAPERS

CONCLUDING OUR TWO PART INTERVIEW WITH NEW CENTRE MANAGER JANE LEWIS:

LOG: With the forthcoming budget round, how well do you think the Oasis will fare?

"It's too soon to tell. We've identified the levels of income and expenditure and as a centre we must work hard to achieve these. The Quarterly Reviews will enable us to identify problem areas early on – both at the Oasis and other sites."

LOG: The "recovery" has been much heralded by the Leisure Industry, do you think there will be a tangible effect on Oasis figures?

"In the short term its inevitable our figures will increase over the summer months. The irony is while most of the industry hopes for fine weather, for us the wetter the better our attendances, except for golf! With the increased promotion on the Oasis as a family day out we will hopefully reach out and attract new target audiences over the coming months"

LOG: What's the Centre Manager's guide to a relaxing weekend, and how did your milestone celebrations go?

"I like to get away at weekends or do something sporty or active, I particularly like camping and surfing and I'm the proud owner of a 7"6 mini-mal surf board. My 30th birthday celebrations lasted all weekend, I still feel 22 so the age doesn't make much difference although I don't relish the prospect of joining the thirtysomethings and everything that goes with it!

Important dates for next month ...

5–18th July Great Western Promotion

10 July Big Daddy vs Giant Hatstacks Wrestling

20th July Thamesdown Schools break up for summer

23rd July Oxon schools break up for summer

ALL ABOARD...!

July's issue of Captain's Log sets sail after 30th July copy deadline. Please submit your news, views, gossip and information to Captain's Log c/o Steve Greenwood's tray in the Administration block.

Figure 9.1 contd.

of the MD in presenting the annual report — the cassettes are then distributed around the world to be shown simultaneously in all countries.

Though videos can do a good PR job and are effective if focused on particular themes or changes companies want to bring about, they are only one-way communication. They therefore need to be used in conjunction with a briefing meeting, for example.

It should also be noted that larger companies are making use of satellite TV to screen presentations and enable studio audiences in different locations to respond — so TV becomes interactive.

Increasingly, with advances in information technology, companies will use electronic mail to send messages to all employees (assuming they have access to personal computers); also electronic bulletin boards can be used in places like staff cafeteria to display and up-date company messages.[6]

But even without such technology you can keep your messages in your staff's eye. MacDonalds, for example, plays training videos in the staff lounge. You can also use posters to reinforce messages on safety, hygiene or quality.

Encouraging staff commitment

Quality circles
In contrast to team briefing, quality circles are made up of *volunteers* from a cross-section of departments who come together to recognise, analyse and solve quality and work-related problems.[7]

Circles consist of between four and a dozen members whose leader has been trained to help the group make recommendations for improvement. Though the process has been perfected in Japan the man who started it was an American, W. E. Deming who in the 1950s was unable to persuade his countrymen to take on board his ideas so he took them to Japan — the rest is history! Perhaps it is not surprising that the US in the 1950s was not disposed to the idea that quality is not about control of output which is inspected but about a *process* of continual improvement which the workforce owned themselves. This is the Japanese concept *kaizen*; kai means 'change' and zen means 'good' (for the better).[8]

Forty years on another word has become popular — 'empowerment' — the commitment of an organisation to give their employees whatever resources and support are needed to achieve a task which they own and control.[19] Given an organisation *has* such a culture quality circles can flourish but where such commitment is lacking — like so many other HRM initiatives — they will not survive. Quality circles are only the means towards an end — that end is often described as TQM (Total Quality Management) — which is the creation of just such a culture where everyone is committed to quality improvement.

Among our case studies it is not surprising that such circles are most developed in the **Oasis Leisure Centre**, which was the first leisure centre to be awarded the BS kite mark for quality assurance BS5750. But other companies are investigating the possibilities.

There are two possibilities I suggest it opens up for the leisure industry: first, the *process* for tapping into the key strengths of a very diverse work-force whose everyday involvement with customers gives them a unique view; second, it requires different staff with different skills to work together as a team. It is towards team formation that we now turn.

Creative teams

As organisations become flatter and managers' span of control increases managers will depend more and more on teams becoming autonomous, to set their own tasks and control procedures and not to be dependent on a supervisor or manager monitoring their every move. This is the agenda for the nineties but understandably many managers who have been brought up in a culture of hierarchy and accountability are anxious about losing control. Lawrence Murrell, Managing Director of **Torquay Leisure Hotel Group**, was one such manager:

> *I wanted to be the boss but gradually the realisation dawned that by involving people, much more can be achieved… The future lies in quality and you can only get at quality by involving everyone and getting them to work as a team.*

To be effective, team members need to pay attention to two underlying functions: the achievement of a task and the maintenance of social and supportive processes that keep the team together. Some people are better at one function than the other. In an influential book Belbin identified no less than eight different roles team members could take each of which was necessary for an effective team.[9] In addition to a chairperson to co-ordinate activities the team needed, for example, 'plants' to supply ideas, 'resource investigators' to seek outside contacts, 'shapers' to report on pattern of events, 'monitor-evaluators' to assess the viability of different ideas and 'completer-finishers' to focus the team on an end result. The rest, 'company workers' and 'teamworkers' got on with the job and ensured everyone got on with each other.

Of late, attention has been focused on the danger of teams (and indeed companies for that matter) becoming too cosy,[10] and the need for 'creative tension' to engender a 'state of inquiry [which] enables us to spot the tough questions that haven't been asked yet'. The need for a stage of what he called 'storming' was identified almost thirty years ago by Tuckman who suggested every group needed to go through four stages in its development:[11]

- Forming: initial stage when group is uncertain of each other and dependent on the leader.
- Storming: stage of questioning the task, possible conflict and resistance to leader.
- Norming: norms emerge, consensus is reached.
- Performing: group comes together to achieve task in most effective way.

Of course it should be a cyclical process. From time to time there needs to be what one of Honda's co-founders calls 'waigaya sessions' (equivalent to 'hubbub' in English) when anyone in a group, regardless of rank, can suggest a session of straight, hard-hitting discussion when anything can be said and the 'undiscussables' can be put on the table without issues being personalised.[10]

Such an approach presupposes an organisational culture which can allow such openness — some companies prefer to use 'outdoor' events like crossing a stream with only assorted items like rope and oilcans to help to engender 'team spirit'. But in the final analysis 'team spirit' must be home grown and specific to the culture of the organisation. I suggest you can't buy in a package to *give* you team spirit. Without exception there was a tangible sense of team spirit in all our case studies. This is helped by the social nature of the industry and the need for continual co-operation which goes beyond a particular occupational role.

Joint consultation

Joint consultation is a process whereby management seeks the views of employees, usually through their elected representatives, before final decisions are taken. Joint consultative committees (JCCs) became popular in the 1970s but have since declined. Their success depends on quality of decision making, working commitment, management awareness and sensitivity.

Where a company has collective bargaining JCCs work well to fill the gaps not covered by negotiation. Indeed it needs to be recognised that a JCC would not discuss issues that are subject to negotiation.

It also needs to be *seen* to be taken seriously by managers whose senior representatives attend as a matter of priority. Finally, the worker representatives — shop-stewards in the case of a unionised company — need to have the trust of the workforce they represent. They also need to be given sufficient information by management on which they can *be* consulted!

Worker directors and works councils

The idea of non-management employees having a place on the Board of a company, and therefore having both access and the opportunities to share in information and decision making at the highest level, is seen by many as the ultimate in employee participation. Again, the 1970s saw its heyday when the Bullock Committee of Inquiry was set up to recommend *how* a worker director scheme would work taking into account 'the essential role of trade unions and having regard to the interests of the national economy, employees, investors, consumers and company efficiency'. With such a brief it is understandable that it was doomed from the outset though companies like British Steel and the Post Office have at various times introduced it, on the whole, successfully. The problem is that employers, workers themselves and trade unionists each have their own reasons for not being that committed to it.

However the implications of what is known as the EC Fifth Directive (*see* also Chapter 2) may force employers to develop a common view. If enacted it would require member states to choose from a number of options for the installation of formal systems to involve employee representatives in company decision-making structures. Luckily for the UK it would allow the possibility of participation through collective agreements rather than Board membership provided that representatives would have the same rights and information as Board members.

The proposals for European Work Councils (EWCs) are a product of the 1990s. These were proposed as part of the need for harmonisation through the Social Chapter. The proposal is that in organisations with at least 1,000 employees and at least two establishments in at least two member states — each of which has at least 100 employees — representatives would be free to request the formation of a European Works Council and participation in wide range of issues. It is unlikely that a Conservative Government would encourage the implementation of such a proposal but one-third of EC firms affected by this proposal are UK-owned. There might therefore be pressure on them to set up EWCs. Equally, EC companies based here would give opportunity to UK employees to share in such councils — if their experience was favourable, it may influence other companies to set up similar systems.

Suggestion schemes

A number of our case studies had staff suggestion schemes. It is important that every suggestion is logged and acknowledged and that the proposer is told what action, if any, has resulted from their idea. If it is taken up then the proposer should receive some kind of reward, be publicly acknowledged in the in-house journal, etc.

Like most other methods it needs to be seen as part of a company-wide strategy for improvement. Land Rover, for example, has a suggestion scheme whereby each person on average turns in 3.2 ideas a year .[12] According to the UK Association of Suggestion Schemes this compares with one in ten of British employees handing in one proposal on average each year. The reason it is so good is because it is part of a wider scheme called RISE (Recognition of Involvement Scheme for Employees), whereby staff get points for just *membership* of a quality action group and more points for having an acceptable suggestion and even more points for giving a group presentation about their suggestion. Points can be converted to cash prizes and other benefits. Staff suggestions have come a long way from dubious notes being passed under the Personnel Manager's door to being an integrated part of an organisation's reward package.

Attitude surveys

It is estimated that about one-third of all large companies in the UK carry out some form of opinion survey.[13] It is a powerful way of finding out what your employees think about their job, company, etc., *but* like everything else, a company has to take it very seriously.

> *The act of conducting a survey has an effect on employee attitudes, regardless of its content. It amounts to a message to employees that their views are considered important, so any subsequent failure either to explain or take action on the results is likely to generate cynicism.*[14]

As we shall see in Chapter 10 the conducting of an employee survey is a key part of the Investor in People scheme.

There are other ways of getting a quick 'picture' (literally) of how staff view themselves, their job, etc., by asking them to put their feelings into a drawing! Hampshire County Council invited staff to draw pictures to describe how they saw their department before and after introduction of a change programme.[15] For example, before the change someone might indicate the 'compartmentalised' way they saw the department in terms of a closed train with non-connecting carriages. This method of getting staff to describe jobs and the organisations is vividly described in a book by Gareth Morgan on 'Imaginisation'.[16]

It takes honesty and courage if you *really* want to find out what staff think, to know about their jobs. Federal Express Business Logistics gets work groups to rate their manager and the company by a simple tick box form which is identical for every employee from lorry driver to MD (survey feedback action). They have to respond to statements like 'My manager lets me know what's expected of me' and 'Working for Federal Express will probably lead to the kind of future I want'. Forms are sent off for computer analysis and then each manager has to have a feedback session with the group and explore problems (if any) underpinning the responses. Compare this approach with Nationwide, where senior managers are expected to attend local briefing meetings and to be challenged by staff and videos are made of proceedings.[2]

Our conclusion is that there is plenty of evidence of companies opening up their communication process so that it is genuinely two-way. Our case studies also show that in addition to the normal top-down methods of communicating they are encouraging staff to make their feelings known. (For the code of practice on participation see reference [18].)

9.4 Examples of good practice

Oasis Leisure Centre

Meetings

Figure 9.2 below shows the range of briefing meetings that meet during the course of the year.

TYPE	WHO ATTENDS	OUTCOME
1. Management Team meeting (monthly)	Centre Manager & Department & Section Heads	Sections report on developments
2. 'Morning Prayers' Weekly — half hour	Centre Manager & Section Heads	Informal weekly review of last week and plan for next
3. Quarterly Quality System Management	All managers/ supervisors	Reviews action on Quality Plan Review
4. Section Heads Quarterly/monthly meeting with staff	Respective section staff	Reviews section issues
5. Activities Manager weekly meeting	Manager with Assistant Managers	Reviews section issues
6. Daily Shift meeting	At start of Shift Duty Officer meets with Catering Supervisor, Technical Assistant & Head Receptionist	Co-ordinates activities
7. Annual Full Staff Meeting	All staff	Review last year & plans for next year

Figure 9.2 Team briefing/communication meetings at Oasis Leisure

In addition there are six quality improvement teams (QITs) each one addressing a particular area of the business, e.g. marketing, facilities, cleaning, etc. They are made up of a cross-section of staff across all departments. The proposals from each QIT are written up and fed into the Centre's Quarterly Review of Quality.

Other forms of communication

- A weekly information sheet giving special events of every day.
- Each staff receives a copy of the Centre's: usage Analysis every month.
- Bi-monthly staff newspaper 'Captain's Log' (see Figure 9.1).

Beaulieu

- Monday morning meeting between MD and Department Heads.
- Department Heads brief staff.
- Thursday 'lunch-in' — wine and cheese get-together — more informal contact between Heads of Department.
- Weekly bulletin 'Newsline'.

Pleasureland

During the season a monthly briefing meeting between the MD and full-time staff which is written up in the form of a 'bulletin' which is circulated to all staff. Recently the MD has tried a different approach — rather than going in with a fixed agenda he has used some meetings not as briefing meetings but as opportunities to hear from staff what *they* would like to discuss. He has been amazed at the difference this makes — after staff have got used to the idea!

The company has also tried to involve seasonal staff by sending out a questionnaire to a sample of staff to get 'their attitudes and opinions concerning their roles'. Here are some examples from the 24 questions posed:

> *The company wishes to promote the 'proud and motivated workforce' image. How do you think the company can achieve this?*
>
> *Do you feel you need any more training for your role at Pleasureland that you haven't already had? What type?*
>
> *Does your section have any form of team briefing session whereby you are briefed by your manager on up and coming events/important decisions? If yes, how are these sessions delivered and at what frequency?*
>
> *Do you feel your managers are approachable and do they actually listen to your ideas/problems?*

Finally there is a 'brainwaves' suggestion scheme open to all staff for ideas 'to save money, improve conditions and performance of workers or increase business' which can earn for the proposer a £100–£1000 cash prize.

Butlins Southcoast World

As one of its guiding principles it has 'communication — which must be fast, open and often'. Central to its strategy is a cascade system of briefing. Every Friday the Centre Director meets with Department Heads and briefs them on items cascaded down from Butlins' MD together with domestic issues. Heads of Department then have to brief their own staff and so on until all staff are briefed; they then report back at the next Friday Executive meeting.

There is a national JCC (Joint Consultative Committee) which meets four times a year to which the centre sends three representatives. The centre has its own local management JCC, with two representatives from each department which meets monthly and a staff representative committee from each department (voted by their peers), which meets monthly.

In addition there are special project groups (health and safety, TQM, etc.).

There is a staff magazine 'Cheers', which appears twice a year and includes in its report findings from regular customer surveys into quality of food, accommodation, etc.

From time to time all staff would receive a copy of a management 'flyer' which gives special news of congratulations for tasks well done or, if necessary, warnings about conduct which needs to be improved.

There is a staff suggestion scheme; suggestions are made on forms and posted via six post boxes situated around the centre. Each one is logged and acknowledged and sent to the appropriate Head of Department who advises if it should go forward for consideration to the Executive Board. Depending on whether an idea is actioned staff can get from £15 to a percentage of the saving or revenue. They also receive a certificate of merit. There is also a 'green scheme' for ideas on improving the environment and prospect of £50 reward.

Every staff member leaving is given an exit interview and reasons for leaving given appear in the annual report.

Bolton Health Studio

Every six weeks they hold what is called a 'breakfast meeting' to which all staff are invited. Though there is an agenda staff have the opportunity to raise any issue they wish.

Museum of the Moving Image

The Manager has a meeting with each shift of actors every week.

Torquay Leisure Hotels

- Annual presentation by MD to all staff.
- Senior Management Team meetings once a month.
- Supervisors in each hotel meet weekly/fortnightly.
- Heads of Department and supervisors meet with all staff every three months.
- In-house staff journal published bi-monthly.

9.5 Lessons to be learned

1. The communication system used is appropriate to the size and culture of the respective organisation. Thus a cascade of team briefings is appropriate to the **Oasis Leisure Centre** whereas 'breakfast meetings' and 'wine and cheese lunchtime' sessions are appropriate to **Bolton Health Studio** and **Beaulieu**. (Though the Centre Manager at the **Oasis** values very much what she calls her weekly informal 'morning prayers' meeting with Department Heads which she says is 'vital'.)

2. In general, team briefings are appropriate to the industry because of the need to make staff aware of coming events very quickly. But companies are increasingly appreciating the need for using such meetings to encourage staff to put forward their own ideas.

9.6 Action Plan

In your Action Plan you will find another check-list for you to complete against the various methods of communication and staff involvement we have described in section 9.3.

1. Identify which methods you use/don't use and note under Comments how you could use or improve your use of method in future or why it would not be appropriate.

2. Read down the list and notes you have made again and star those methods which you think should be introduced as a matter of urgency and commit yourself to take action Make a note against each as to whether you use it at the moment and what would be an argument for *or against* using it in the future.

9.7 References

1. Andrews, N. (1993) *Your Employees: Your Edge in the 1990s: II* Smythe Dorward Lambert.

2. Pickard, J. (1993) When employees answer back *Personnel Management Plus* Vol. 4, No. 9, September 1993, pp. 20–21.

3. Marchington, M., Wilkinson, A. and Ackers, P. (1993) Waving or drowning in participation *Personnel Management* March 1993, pp. 46–50.

4. Fowler, A. (1991) How to keep employees informed *Personnel Management Plus* Vol. 2, No.10, October 1991, pp. 25–26.

5. Grummit, J. (1983) *Team Briefing* Industrial Society.

6. Smith, A. (1993) Screen test *Personnel Management* 23 February 1993.

7. Robson, M. (1984) *Quality Circles in Action* Gower.

8. Walker, V. (1993) Kaizen — the art of continual improvement *Personnel Management* August 1993.

9. Belbin, M. (1981) *Management Teams: Why they succeed or fail* Heinemann

10. Pascale, R. (1993) The benefit of a clash of opinions *Personnel Management* October 1993, pp. 38–41.

11. Tuckman, B. (1965) Development sequences in small groups *Psychological Bulletin* 63.

12. Pickard, J. (1993) Handling proper suggestions on the shopfloor *Personnel Management Plus* Vol. 3, No. 4, 1993, pp. 14–15.

13. Williams, M. (1993) Fair comment *Personnel Today* 9 March 1993.

14. Fowler, A. (1993) How to plan and use attitude surveys *Personnel Management Plus* Vol. 4, No. 6, p. 25, June 1993.

15. Lisney, B. and Allen, C. (1993) Taking a snapshot of cultural change *Personnel Management* February 1993.

16. Morgan, G. (1993) *Imaginization — The Art of Creative Management* Sage.

17. Hilton, P. (1992) Letting staff express themselves *Personnel Management Plus* Vol. 3, No. 5, May 1993.

18. Involvement and Participation Association/Institute of Personnel Management (1990) *Employee Involvement and Participation in the United Kingdon: the IPA/IPM Code.*

19. Pickard, J. (1993) The real meaning of empowerment *Personnel Management* November 1993.

10. Becoming recognised as an investor in people

10.1 The principles

The scheme known as 'Investor in People' was the result of preliminary work by the National Training Task Force (NTTF) — established by the 1988 White Paper 'Employment for the Nineties' to find ways to encourage companies to develop staff — and the CBI. The NTTF spent a year talking to successful businesses and finding out what were the *people* factors that made one company more successful than another. The key factor was that successful companies communicated business goals to staff and then proceeded to give them the support and development needed to achieve them. This is the essence of the Investor in People national standard which was launched at the CBI conference in 1990 and piloted before being formally launched on 16 October 1991.

The national standard comprises four key principles each of which can be assessed against specific 'indicators' which indicate evidence needed to satisfy the standard. Not surprisingly Edward Fennell sees it as a kind of NVQ for organisations.[1]

In your Action Plan each of the four principles together with all 24 indicators have been reproduced with the kind permission of Investors in People UK. Many of them should be familiar to you as we have introduced a number of them in the course of helping you build up your HRM strategy. Indeed, the hope is that if you have taken on board the principles of each chapter so far and completed your Action Plan to-date you should have more than enough evidence to support an application for IiP (*see* section 10.3). Against each indicator there is a reference to chapters in the book which are relevant to the respective indicator.

The four principles are deceptively simple:

- *Commitment:* A public commitment from the senior manager to communicate a vision and plan of where the company is going and to develop all employees to contribute to and achieve the company's goals.
- *Planning:* A review of the training needs to be made to achieve the goals and make the necessary resources available.
- *Action:* To train every employee as necessary on recruitment and thereafter facilitate the individual development of every employee throughout their employment.
- *Evaluation:* To evaluate the investment in training and development at all levels against business goals and targets.

Clearly some chapters in the book are more relevant than others as the focus of IiP is on training and development. But, as we suspect companies applying for IiP soon discover, training policy cannot exist in a vacuum — it has to evolve from the unique culture of the organisation which, as we have seen is shaped by a whole range of HRM policies — recruitment, selection, reward and above all, by the way the organisation communicates these polices. Even the way an organisation signals its concerns for and communicates its commitment to individuals' rights under the law can make a difference.

Interestingly each of our three case studies which have successfully met the Investor standard did not start out cold to implement training and development. In each case a senior manager recognised that what IiP had to offer matched a stage of development that the company had *already* reached and helped provide a strategic framework within which further development could take place.

For the MD of **Torquay Leisure Hotels Group** his introduction to IiP coincided with a major shift in his own philosophy (*see* Chapter 9) and change in management style. For him IiP was a perfect vehicle for opening up communication and ownership of targets by groups of staff. Only *then* could training and development have the impact IiP was seeking to identify. It was awarded IiP in November 1992.

For the Personnel and Training Executive of **Butlins Southcoast World**, IiP fitted perfectly into his strategy for introducing NVQ assessment. His aim was to effect a change of culture whereby everyone assumed personal and professional responsibility which was recognised and rewarded. IiP was a natural development and offered a framework within which individual development could be linked to business goals. The company was awarded IiP status in July 1992.

In late 1991 the Director and General Manager of **Pleasureland** launched 'the Year of Quality', the purpose of which was to 'put the notion of improvement and therefore change in peoples' minds'. It was the start of a process but what was the next stage? In 1992 he attended the launch presentation of IiP which seemed to offer what he was looking for, namely a framework for the *people* side of the business which was linked to quality. The company was awarded IiP status in August 1993.

In all cases, therefore, Investor in People was seen as a strategic tool to further initiatives that had *already* taken place. This is why we have not revealed until now the full range of IiP indicators. Our purpose is that you first have an opportunity to review the HRM culture in which your organisation *presently* operates. Having done that, you are now in a position to review how IiP can *continue* and *consolidate* the development process you should already have started through actions you have committed yourself to in the Action Plan.

You should also be aware of criticisms of the scheme:

1. *Targets out of range* — the Government's target is 50 per cent of all medium-sized companies (more than 200 employees) to be certified as investors by 1996. An Industry Society survey of 400 employers finds that 50 per cent have no intention of applying.[2] Currently 3,000 companies are reported as committed.

2. *Wrong reason for applying* — Gibbons suggests that it is the larger companies and those associated with TEC Board members who are the first to apply.[3]

3. *Political pressure* — TECs funding depends on reaching targets of getting companies up to IiP. TECs had to persuade one in four companies with more than 200 staff to draw up an Action Plan by 1994. Against this there is a need for *time* to get sufficient experience. The question arises, therefore, as to whether quality will suffer.

4. *Inconsistency of assessment between TECs* — to counteract this criticism, TECs in the North-west, for example, have established a common approach to assessment to maintain standards and control costs and establish a pool of their own fully qualified assessors.

5. *Too bureaucratic* — time pressure and bureaucracy involved were the two top reasons identified by the Industry Society survey for employers not to apply for IiP.[2] Against this it has to be said that the tool-kit is reasonably easy to use. Also, as with NVQ assessment, one piece of evidence can meet requirements of more than one indicator.

6. *Standard diminished if numbers of companies Government is targeting get it?*

7. *Geared towards company needs rather than individual development needs* — this is reflected in the employee survey where the employee has simply to respond YES/NO whereas the manager analysis is much more detailed. Also, the employee survey is optional.

Only you can decide if it is worth the investment. Our argument is that if you are truly interested in introducing an HRM approach to the development of your staff as this book has advocated then you should not just be able to meet the criteria you should exceed them (*see* Conclusions).[4]

10.2 What's in it for me?

1. IiP is a nationally recognised standard of a company's commitment to develop its people in relation to its business goals. As such, rather like BS 5750, it is likely to become a nationally recognised standard of good practice which employees and potential recruits and *customers* will *demand* a company meets.

2. There is evidence that in implementing IiP standards a company can expect improved profitability, a competitive marketing advantage and a more committed and adaptable workforce.[5] As the business improves, a greater proportion of staff are retained and overall commitment of workforce improves.

   For the record **Torquay Leisure Hotel** reports the following benefits since being awarded IiP:
   - Gross profit has increased by 25 per cent between 1990–1992.
   - Recruitment costs down by 60 per cent.
   - 95 per cent customer satisfaction.
   - High level of repeat business.

   Butlins Southcoast World reports on:
   - Recruitment and training costs reduced.
   - Reduction in staff turnover.
   - Staff-related customer complaints reduced.
   - Improved motivation and team work.

   Pleasureland reports on:
   - Complete turnaround in staff recruitment problems — now have waiting list of staff wanting to work for them.
   - Individual sense of ownership and commitment.
   - Much improved communication between departments.
   - Evidence that pay is not biggest factor in recruitment.

3. Though completion of written evidence is involved, meeting the requirements is essentially *practical* and should be in line with the action a company intends to take anyway.

10.3 *What's involved?*

Stage 1 — Deciding if you're ready for IiP

1. Apply to your local TEC for a copy of the National set of Guides on Investor in People. These give you a breakdown of the four key criteria and 24 indicators (which are reproduced in the final pages of your Action Plan) together with practical advice on how to go about applying for assessment. The main Guides are as follows:

   - A brief for top managers.
   - How do we measure up?
   - How do we move forward?
   - How will we gain recognition?
   - Evaluating your investment in people?
   - Investing in people: the payoff.

   There are also Guides aimed at the small business.

2. Use the Guide 'How do we measure up?' to carry out a survey of managers and employees to find how you currently match up to the IiP standards. Figure 10.1 shows sample questions from each of the surveys.

Manager Survey Questions (Participants are asked to rate each statement from A to D according to extent to which there is current evidence for it .)

- 'People at all levels in the organisation know how they can contribute to our success.'
- 'Our plans clearly identify the resources which we will use to meet training and development needs.'

Employee Survey Questions (Participants merely asked to answer YES/NO.)

- 'Are your training and development needs reviewed regularly?'
- 'Has your immediate manager communicated to you the organisation's broader aims or vision?'

Figure 10.1 Sample questions from the IiP Guide 'How do we measure up?'

As a result of carrying out these surveys you will be able to identify where you fall down against IiP indicators. You can then either decide to carry on and commit yourself to an Action Plan to remedy deficiencies identified or decide that IiP is not for you. Whatever you decide, we suggest that simply by carrying out a survey of management and staff attitudes will reveal some interesting trends (and differences of perception!). You can also apply to the TEC for an advisor to carry out a 'health check' (for which, of course, you would have to pay).

Stage 2 — Signifying your commitment

3. If you decide to apply for IiP, the TEC needs a letter from the most senior manager in the organisation indicating their commitment to the process of IiP which will have been communicated to all employees. It should reflect a commitment to training and development of all, similar to what should be contained in your Training Policy (*see* Figure 6.3, Chapter 6).

4. Accompanying the letter there should be an Action Plan which summarises action that needs to be taken, by whom and by when — against each IiP indicator where survey/health check indicated a shortfall of some kind.

Stage 3 — Implementing the action plan

5. It is the responsibility of the senior manager (who signed the commitment letter) to ensure that people identified in the Action Plan now implement the necessary steps indicated in the plan.

6. The outcomes of the Action Plan should be reflected in the form of evidence which is put together in a portfolio (very similar to the process of summarising evidence for assessment against NVQs — in Chapter 3). Just as NVQ standards advise you what kind of evidence should be collected, so the IiP tool-kit gives you examples of the kind of evidence that will be required to satisfy each indicator. You will also need to provide a summary sheet which indicates what item of evidence meets each indicator. Figure 10.2 shows an extract from the summary sheet to **Pleasureland**'s portfolio of evidence. It details evidence in the portfolio that relates to indicator 1.2.

1.2: Employees at all levels are aware of the broad aims or vision of the organisation

See 1.1 for Mission statement.

Memorandum (12th July 1992) to all permanent employees below supervisor level.

Memorandum (12th July) to all managers and supervisors.

Initial Employee survey (12th August 1992).

Initial management survey (12th August 1992).

Report to Main Board of Directors (16th September 1992).

Memorandum (5th October 1992) re-presentation to all Managers.

Presentation script used 12th October 1992 for presentation to Managers and Supervisors.

**Figure 10.2 Extract from Pleasureland's portfolio of evidence
from its Action Plan**

At any time during this process you can be helped by an adviser appointed by the TEC. Charges per day would range from £200-£500.

Stage 3 — Assessment

7. When you (and your adviser) consider you are ready for assessment you make a formal application to the TEC which then appoints an independent assessor. They will initially inspect the contents of your portfolio.

8. As a result of an analysis of the portfolio it is likely that questions will arise which the assessor needs to check out on-site, when they will want to talk to managers,

specialists and, most importantly, a sample of employees. These are typical questions that might be asked:

- 'Tell me what is the purpose of your job?'
- 'What training have you had?'

Stage 4 — Recognition

9. As a result of reviewing the evidence the assessor makes a formal report which they present to the TEC IiP Recognition Panel. At this stage it is the assessor rather than the company who is quizzed to ensure evidence is up to IiP standards. If it agrees the company is recognised as an Investor in People, is allowed to use the IiP logo (*see* Figure 10.3) on its notepaper and receives a plaque for display.

Figure 10.3 Investor in People logo

If it is agreed that the company does not meet the criteria, it will receive the necessary feedback to enable it to make a subsequent application

Stage 5 — Reassessment

10. After three years the organisation must reapply and the process begins all over again. In this case the assessor would be looking for evidence of the company's continual improvement of standards and response to new developments. The first round of reassessments will take place in 1994.

Time taken to become an investor ranges to-date from 5–20 months.

10.4 Examples of good practice

We have already illustrated above why three of our case studies were motivated to apply for IiP, the benefits they have found since and the process they went through to get it. For a detailed summary of how **Torquay Leisure Hotel Group** obtained IiP see Critten's overview.[6]

10.5 Lessons to be learned

1. All three case studies confirm above that they didn't start from scratch. Each had already embarked on an HRM initiative to improve the development of their staff. The Investor in People framework provided them with a way of developing further initiatives already started. The Action Plan you have so far produced should be the basis on which you can now assess yourself against IiP criteria.

2. In addition to the fundamental principle of being able to demonstrate that every employee is being trained or developed in line with organisational goals all three case studies reaffirmed importance of three central support *processes:*
    - the need for an appraisal scheme covering *all* employees
    - open communication system in which *every* member of staff can participate
    - a means by which every development activity can be *evaluated* against measurable criteria.

3. The achievement of the IiP award has not stopped any of the companies developing further. Indeed after the current Government pressure for *getting* IiP subsides the more important question to ask is: where do companies go from here? See Critten (1993)[4,6] for details of how to build on IiP.

10.6 Action Plan

In your Action Plan you will find a grid which lists all of the 24 indicators that need to be satisfied to obtain an Investor in People award. All that remains now is for you to look back at the Action Plan you have produced so far and assess yourself against each criterion. You might then get an independent view from staff and management — after all, if you apply for IiP you will be required to carry out such a survey.

As we have suggested above, the Plan you should have produced as a result of going through this book should exceed what is required by IiP (in areas like reward management and staff rights for example). In the Conclusions section at the end of the book, we summarise the potential for companies in the leisure industry to become not just Investors in People but Learning Organisations.

10.7 References

1. Fennell, E. (1992) Investors in People: what's it got to do with NVQs? *Competence and Assessment* No. 19, pp. 10–11.

2. Industrial Society (1992) *Training Trends* No. 7, Winter 1992/3.

3. Gibbons, A. (1992) IIP — a trainer's concerns *Training and Development (UK)* Vol. 10, No. 11, November 1992, pp. 17–18.

4. Critten, P. (1993) *Investing in People: Towards Corporate Capability* Butterworth Heinemann

5. Employment Department (1993) *Investing in People— The Benefits of being an Investor in People* Employment Department, April 1993.

6. Critten, P. (1993) Investing in people to become a learning organisation *ILAM Guide to Good Practice in Leisure Management* Longman.

Individual Action Plan

Chapter 1 Mission/strategy/culture/structure

1. The purpose of my organisation

2. Compare above purpose with that emerging from work groups. Agree revised definition

3. Collect together statements of core values and combine together to form a Vision statement of what it is like to work for your organisation

4. How would you describe your organisational culture now and how it should be

5. In what form of structure do people currently work (See Figure 1) and what would be the most appropriate structure to realise the mission and values as described in 1 and 2

Chapter 2 Rights, responsibilities and procedures

1. Carry out an audit of the mix of staff and contractual arrangements under following headings

	% staff	
	Male	Female

• Full Time
• Part Time
• Seasonal contract
• Age 16 – 21
    22 – 30
    31 – 40
    40 – 50
    50+
• Registered disabled
• Ethnic origin outside UK/EC
• In supervisor/manager role		

2. Carry out audit of how well you match up to current employment legislation

	HOW WELL COVERED	CHANGES TO BE MADE	HOW TO BE COMMUNICATED
1. CONTRACT OF EMPLOYMENT • Essential information covered in one document & communicated within 2 months of starting? • Supplementary information communicated within 2 months? **2. DISCRIMINATION** Evidence that no one is discriminated against in selection and employment on following grounds • Being a trade union member • Sex • Race • Past offender • Disabled **3. MATERNITY RIGHTS** • Policy on • Rate of Statutory Maternity Pay			

	HOW WELL COVERED	CHANGES TO BE MADE	HOW TO BE COMMUNICATED
4. HEALTH & SAFETY • HASAWA provisions • COSSH • Fire precautions • Social Charter directives			
5. UNFAIR DISMISSAL & REDUNDANCY • Policy on 'reasonableness' • Disciplinary procedure • Policy on redundancy • Rate of pay • Support provided			
6. TRADE UNIONS • What, if any, recognised • How contribute to HRM strategy			
7. EC CHARTER Implications of • Freedom of movement • Employment & remuneration • Information, consultation & participation • Protection of children/ adolescents • Elderly • Disabled			

Chapter 3 Redefining jobs and recognising competence at work

1. What are the key functions your organisation needs to undertake to achieve the mission described in Chapter 1?

2. As a result of carrying out a functional analysis (for details see Chapter 3) what are the core competences needed at work?

3. Find out what NVQs are available that cover similar functions (See Figure 5) and acquire copy from appropriate Lead Body (or contact ILAM 0491 87422)

4. Compare these NVQs and competences you have identified yourself with tasks/responsibilities as defined on existing job description. Are they covered? Could they be described in different format that better reflect key competences needed? (Look at Figures 2,3 and 4 in Chapter 3)

5. Identify who in organisation is best suited to train (See Chapter 6) and assess against competences (Chapter 7)

6. Test out validity of competences as basis for recruitment (Chapter 4), selection (Chapter 5), training and development (Chapter 6), appraisal (Chapter 7) and as a basis for rewarding staff (Chapter 8)

Chapter 4 Targeted recruitment

1. Remind yourself of the mission statement and core values you arrived at following Chapter 1. Describe below the profile of staff that are likely to achieve this mission.

2. Now look back at the two audits you carried out of composition of staff currently employed and legal implications after Chapter 2. What are implications for recruiting a different mix of staff on a different contractual basis?

3. Look at the competence profile you drew up at the end of chapter 3. What specific competences do you need to recruit in the future?

4. Devise a Job Advertisement targeting a particular group of staff to fill any position of your choice that takes account of above criteria

Chapter 5 Opening up selection

1. List all information you have about job/role being selected — draw on information from Action Plan following chapters 3 and 4 — and draw up Person Specification

2. Check that application form (if used) provides information as listed above.

3. From applications received draw up short-list of 6–8 who best meet criteria

4. Compile a matrix identifying appropriate testing technique that is appropriate to each competence/cy identified (See Figure 3)

5. Keep record of result of each assessment technique used and ensure each candidate is very clear about criteria against which they are being assessed and that they receive feedback (whether successful or not)

6. Have candidates who have not been successful been told as soon after selection process as is possible?

Chapter 6 A policy for training, development and continuous learning

1. List core competences that have to be covered company wide (Refer back to Chapter 3). Against each competence identify current training method for achieving it and then consider alternative methods that could be used

COMPETENCES	TRAINING/DEVELOPMENT METHOD FOR ACHIEVING	ALTERNATIVE METHODS

2. Review training courses/events currently offered and beside each identify how you would assess evidence of learning being applied in workplace

COURSE/LEARNING EVENT OBJECTIVE	EVIDENCE OF APPLICATION AT WORK

3. On record sheet that follows identify individuals needing induction, job specific and continuing development over the next year

TRAINING PLAN			YEAR		
INDUCTION					
Numbers	Dates	Resources needed			Cost
JOB-SPECIFIC					
Staff	Description	Who responsible	Method	Date	Cost
ON-GOING DEVELOPMENT					
Staff	Description	Who responsible	Method	Date	Cost

Chapter 7 Appraising and evaluating performance

1. Carry out exercise described in Action Points 1-4 and write down below the degree of unity between assessor and 'assessee'

2. For each functional group/team in your organisation get the respective supervisor/manager to ask each member of the team to respond to the eight questions in Action Point 7 and then agree with team leader a common set of criteria. Write down below what this tells you about your organisation.

3. Ask each group to draw up their own self-assessment sheet which enables them to measure themselves against criteria agreed in 2

4.   Having collected in assessment sheets from all groups and agreed with team leaders any other criteria which reflect company goals, draw up format for an appraisal form that can be used with all staff company-wide. NB Before being put into practice it should be checked out again through the functional groups

Chapter 8 Paying for performance and reward management

1. Use the following questions to survey attitudes of a representative group of staff (ie representative of different levels, full-time/part-time. seasonal)

   1. Do you know the base rate at which you are paid?

   2. How familiar are you with pay rates/scales for other staff?

   3. In what ways, if at all, are you rewarded for meeting specified performance criteria/ targets?

   4. Do you receive any bonus for performance within a team?

   5. Do you get any bonus from company as a whole?

   6. What other non-financial benefits do you get?

   7. What non-financial benefits does the company provide? (Eg discount on meals, holidays, gifts etc) How are these related to performance?

   8. If you were able to design your own ideal reward package what would it contain?

2. Use matrix below to compile a picture of how you reward different groups of staff

GROUP JOBS TO DIFFERENTIATE BETWEEN BENEFITS (e.g. seasonal, FT, Managers, operational, clerical)
1. BASE RATES — salary bands (based on job evaluation?) — hourly pay
2. INDIVIDUAL PERFORMANCE RELATED PAY — Increases on merit — individual bonus
3. GROUP PERFORMANCE RELATED PAY — Target related — Gainshare
4. COMPANY PERFORMANCE RELATED PAY — Profit share — Other share schemes
5. CAFETERIA OF BENEFITS — Mix
6. INDIVIDUAL GIFTS/INCENTIVES — Describe
7. PAYING FOR SKILLS

3. Write a report detailing your findings and recommendations for an improved reward system including answers to questions posed in Action Point 3

161

Chapter 9 Communicating and involving staff

Consider each of the methods listed below (covered in section 3 of Chapter 9) and beside each identify which methods are currently used, what could be used in future and those methods which are of key importance

HOW WELL AM I COMMUNICATING WITH AND INVOLVING MY STAFF?			
METHOD	USED NOW?	COMMENT ON FUTURE USE	KEY RATING?
Team briefings			
Mass meetings			
One-to-one			
Memoranda/circulars			
Notice boards			
In-house journal			
Annual report			
Video/technology			
Quality circles			
Creative teams			
Joint Consultative Committees			
Worker Directors/Works Councils			
Suggestion schemes			
Attitude surveys			

Chapter 10 Becoming recognised as an investor in people

1.   Assess yourself against the following 24 indicators of investor in people

	HOW SATISFY	ADDITIONAL ACTION NEEDED	REFERENCE TO CHAPTER
1. Commitment			
1.1 There is a public commitment from the most senior level within the organisation to develop people			1, 4, 9
1.2 Employees at all levels are aware of the broad aims or vision of the organisation			1, 4, 9
1.3 There is a written but flexible plan which sets out business goals and targets			1
1.4 The plan identifies broad development needs and specifies how they will be assessed and met			6
1.5 The employer has considered what employees at all levels will contribute to the success of the organisation and has communicated this effectively to them			3, 4
1.6 Where representative structures exist, management communicates with employee representatives a vision of where the organisation is going and the contribution employees (and their representatives) will make to its success			2
2. Planning			
2.1 The written plan identifies the resources that will be used to meet training and development needs			1, 6

	HOW SATISFY	ADDITIONAL ACTION NEEDED	REFERENCE TO CHAPTER
2.2 Training and development needs are regularly reviewed against business objectives			6, 7
2.3 A process exists for regularly reviewing the training development needs of all employees			6, 7
2.4 Responsibility for developing people is clearly identified throughout the organisation, starting at the top			3, 6
2.5 Managers are competent to carry out their responsibilities for developing people			6
2.6 Targets and standards are set for development actions			3, 6
2.7 Where appropriate, training targets are linked to achieving external standards and particularly to National Vocational Qualifications (or Scottish Vocational qualifications in Scotland) and units			3, 6
3. Action			
3.1 All new employees are introduced effectively to the organisation and are given the training and development they need to do the job			4, 5, 6
3.2 The skills of existing employees are developed in line with business objectives			3, 6
3.3 All employees are made aware of the development opportunities open to them			6, 9

	HOW SATISFY	ADDITIONAL ACTION NEEDED	REFERENCE TO CHAPTER
3.4 All employees are encouraged to help identify and meet their job-related development needs			6, 7
3.5 Effective action takes place to achieve the training and development objectives of individuals and the organisation			6
3.6 Managers are actively involved in supporting employees to meet their training and development needs			6, 7
4. Evaluation			
4.1 The organisation evaluates how its development of people is contributing to business goals and targets			6, 7
4.2 The organisation evaluates whether its development actions have achieved their objectives			3, 6, 7
4.3 The outcomes of training and development are evaluated at individual, team and organisational levels			3, 6, 7
4.4 Top management understand the broad costs and benefits of developing people			7, 8
4.5 The continuing commitment of top management to developing people is communicated to all employees			6, 9

Conclusions

Throughout this book we have focused on key changes in the world of work that must inevitably have an impact on Human Resource Management. Changes like flatter organisation, different and flexible patterns of working, emphasis on teamwork, empowerment of staff etc. In the Introduction I suggested that though HRM and Personnel Management literature reflected how different sectors of the market were responding to these changes, reference to the Leisure Industry has been markedly absent. It was and is my hope that the experience recorded in this book of how seven companies from this sector of industry are responding to and initiating change might help to put the record straight. What is more, it seems to me that the Industry is well placed not just to respond to changes but to be a model of the new kind of organisations which will be required for the next century. On the evidence supplied by our seven case studies there are four trends which bode well for the future:

1. *Flexible working practice:* At a time when contract work is becoming the norm rather than the exception and part-time work is likely to increase, the practice of seasonal contracts sets a useful precedent; particularly, if like **Butlins Southcoast World** such staff have the same opportunities as other staff to acquire nationally recognised qualifications and have a career progression path — if they want it — towards full-time work (or, perhaps that should read fuller time work!)

2. *Open Recruitment and Selection practice:* The practice of using Open Days to recruit staff is a very practical way of ensuring potential staff get a feel for the context in which they will be working as well as being able to demonstrate a range of skills which in a more closed recruitment/selection process might never have come to light.

3. *Teamwork:* By its very nature the Leisure Industry depends on good teamwork to ensure the safety and satisfaction of its customers. The evidence suggests that companies are gradually 'empowering' teams to take on more responsibility and rewarding them accordingly.

    In the future this might lead to organisations restructuring the way they work to facilitate this process even more. For example, allowing teams to recruit, train and reward their own staff and agree whatever contractual arrangements best suit them.

4. *Two-way communication:* There is strong evidence that cascading information down the line via team briefings fits into the culture of many organisations (e.g. **Oasis Leisure Centre** and **Butlins Southcoast World**) But at the same time there is evidence that companies are opening up their communication systems sufficiently to encourage and encompass contributions from all levels of staff.

The stress factors identified by Bill Bacon in the Introduction cannot be dismissed but at the same time the evidence of staff commitment from our case-studies shows that providing an organisation creates the appropriate culture the industry can provide opportunities at work which research shows staff are seeking. Contrary to popular opinion these don't revolve around rates of pay (which is just as well for the Leisure Industry!); they do encompass opportunities for training and development and recognition for skills applied and responsibility taken. All of our case studies provide evidence that staff are finding just such opportunities in their own companies. Another theme which has surfaced a number of times during the book is the concept of the 'Learning Organisation' which is an 'Organisation which facilitates the learning of all its members and continuously transforms itself'.[1] Elsewhere I have described how one of our case studies obtained the Investor in People award and I go on to explore further how this might help it to become a Learning Organisation.[2] Now that you have produced an Action Plan which should cover most of the key indicators required by IiP you might want to assess yourself against the following criteria which characterise a learning organisation. Such an organisation:

- has a climate in which all members are encouraged to learn and to develop their full potential
- extends this learning culture to include customers, suppliers and other significant stakeholders
- makes Human Resource Development strategy central to Business Policy
- involves a continuous process of organisational transformation
- is one in which learning and working are synonymous[1]

I hope that as a result of working through the various exercises in this book you are one step further to becoming a Learning Organisation, that you will apply to your local TEC to make a commitment to become an Investor in People and that you will celebrate your success by sharing your experience of HRM with others.

References

1. Pedler, M., Boydell, T. and Burgoyne, J. (1991) *The Learning Company* McGraw Hill.

2. Critten, P. (1993) Investing in People to becoming a learning organisation *ILAM Guide to Good Practice in Leisure Management* Chapter 3.3, Longman.

Index